THE
Mexican
SLOW COOKER

THE
Mexican
SLOW COOKER

RECIPES FOR MOLE, ENCHILADAS,
CARNITAS, CHILE VERDE PORK,
AND MORE FAVORITES

DEBORAH SCHNEIDER

Photography by Maren Caruso

TEN SPEED PRESS

Berkeley

CONTENTS

THANKS · vi

INTRODUCTION · 1

USING THE SLOW COOKER · 3

Soups · 11

Mains and Guisados · 35

Street Food Favorites · 57

Basics, Rice, Beans, and Other Sides · 93

Desserts · 117

INGREDIENTS · 129

INDEX · 134

THANKS

IT TAKES A WHOLE PUEBLO to make a book, and I hereby gratefully acknowledge the support and contributions of *my* village. To Ten Speed Press editor Melissa Moore and designer Chloe Rawlins, thanks for the opportunity to create this book, and for making it beautiful. To my agent and dear friend, Carole Bidnick, no words can express my gratitude for your support and many kindnesses. Thanks to Maren Caruso for creating the most soulful portraits imaginable of this humble food, and to food stylist Kim Kissling and prop stylist Ethel Brennan for getting it ready for prime time. Thanks always to the wonderful crew at Zanzibar in Pacific Beach, for their enthusiasm for the project and their excellent *americanos*.

The best way to get to the heart of Mexico is through its stomach. It's a privilege to introduce my readers to this magnificent country, its food, history, and culture. As always, I want to thank the very special group of people who have shared their knowledge and love of Mexican cooking with me over the years. *Mil gracias*, then, to all my kitchen *compadres* over the years, especially Manny Lopez, Benito Mirafuentes, Joe Saldana, Danny Esparza, and Paul Saiguero from SOL Mexican Cocina, and many others. My profound thanks to the extraordinary Patricia Quintana, a gifted chef and author whose great passion is keeping alive the traditional culinary *patrimonio* of Mexico to pass to a new generation. And *un abrazo* to the charming and knowledgeable Ruth Alegria for sharing her knowledge of Mexico City and demonstrating the finer points of the *vuelta ingles*.

And last, but *certainly* not least, I am very grateful for the enthusiasm and constructive criticism offered by my homegrown group of food critics: Barry, Anne, and Will Schneider, who are more patient with me than I have any right to expect, and my partners and staff at the SOL Mexican Cocinas in Newport Beach and Scottsdale. I am one lucky *güera*.

INTRODUCTION

THE MEXICAN CULINARY HERITAGE is unique. One of the world's most ancient cuisines, Mexican cooking is so important globally that it has been placed on UNESCO's Representative List of the Intangible Cultural Heritage of Humanity. The heart and soul of the Mexican kitchen is the *olla* (sometimes called a *cazuela*), a simple pot of earthenware or metal. Tucked away on the back of the stove, the *olla* is always bubbling away with something delicious whose aroma fills the *casa*, no matter how humble.

While developing the recipes for this book, my fifth on Mexican cooking, I was pleasantly surprised—thrilled, actually—to discover how well traditional Mexican cooking can be adapted to the modern electric slow cooker. That's because a slow cooker is just a type of *olla* in an easy-to-use form. Classic preparations such as *guisados* (stews), tamales, *caldos* (broths), moles, and many other favorites all get their wonderful flavor from long, slow cooking, which tenderizes the meat and infuses simple ingredients with the rich flavors of chiles and vegetables. And with a slow cooker you can just plug it in and go about your business instead of tending the stove for hours.

Some of these recipes require a few steps, such as toasting or charring, in order to obtain authentic Mexican flavors and best results. You will learn these easy techniques as you work your way though the book.

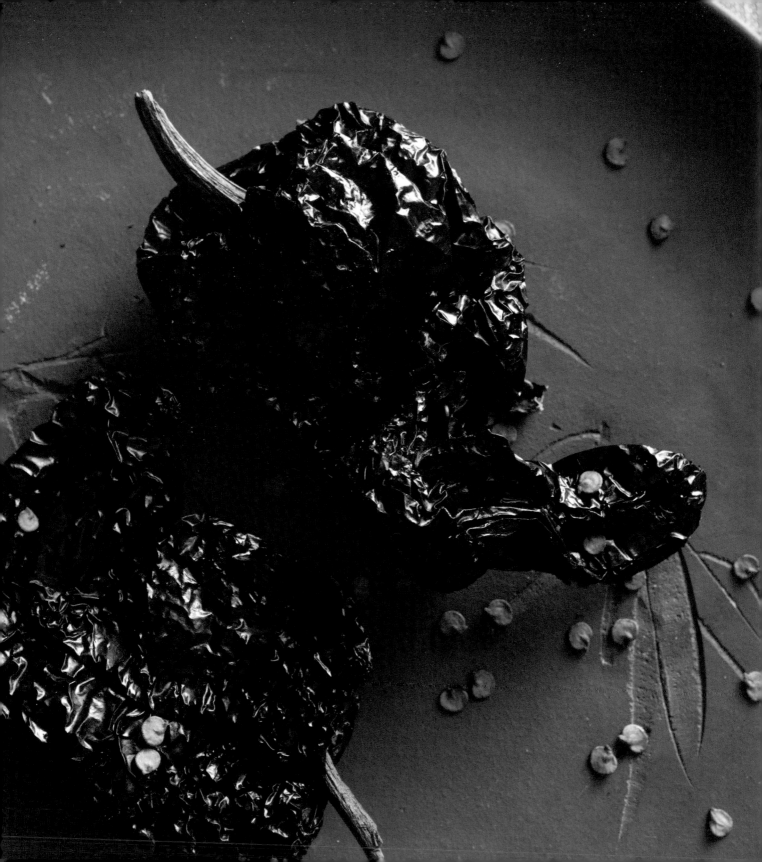

USING THE SLOW COOKER

THE SLOW COOKER IS the perfect convenience for people who live in the fast lane. Instead of relying on convenience foods, which really don't save time (and contain all sorts of additives), you can come home to a house that smells great and enjoy a healthy, delicious homemade meal made with quality ingredients that *you* control. With very little effort you can keep your freezer stocked with the makings of a feast: broths, sauces and salsas, beans and soups, and savory main dishes.

The slow cooker is also remarkably versatile. Not only can you make soups and stews, but you can also use your slow cooker to bake cakes, steam tamales, and transform your countertop into a bain marie. It doubles as a rice cooker and buffet server, and it's smart enough to cook a dish for the correct amount of time and then hold it until you are ready to eat it. Once you learn what your slow cooker can do, it will certainly make your life easier.

An Introduction to Slow Cookers

Slow cookers generally come in 2-, 4-, 5-, 6-, and 7-quart sizes, and they may be oval or round. The shape does not seem to make a difference in how the food cooks.

I developed most of the recipes in this book to serve 4 to 6 people and tested them in a $5\frac{1}{2}$-quart oval cooker with an earthenware insert. Slow cookers are relatively inexpensive, so you may want to own them in several different sizes. Many cooks invest in a 7-quart cooker for making stocks and tamales and cooking for large groups, but they also own a 2-quart cooker to keep food hot at potlucks and parties.

If you are cooking for two, all of the recipes in this book may be halved and made in a 4-quart slow cooker. Even so, you may want to make the full recipe and freeze any leftovers. Why cook twice?

Generally speaking, it's better to cook a smaller amount in a large cooker than to overfill a small cooker. My 5^1/$_2$-quart cooker works beautifully even when it is less than half full.

Slow Cooker Features

Be sure to purchase a slow cooker with an automatic "warm" setting (check carefully, since not all models have this feature). That way, even if you are away all day, the food will stop cooking at the correct time and will be kept warm at a safe temperature until you return. Another terrific feature that I highly recommend is a digital timer, which enables you to set a precise cooking time rather than relying on the standard presets of 4 and 8 hours. Food is often cooked perfectly at 3, 5, or 7 hours.

Although you can now buy slow cookers with metal inserts, which get hot enough to use for browning, I much prefer the results I get from the gentle, even heat of a standard earthenware insert. If I do need to brown something for a recipe, it's easy enough to do it on the stove top. Be sure to scrub the insert and lid thoroughly using a nonscratch scrub pad and soap and water after using them, and air dry them before putting them away.

Cooking Tips

Recipes
Take a moment to read the recipe all the way through before you start to cook. The recipes in this book will satisfy 4 to 6 average appetites. If you are cooking for fewer people, the recipes can be halved to serve 2 or 3, in which case they can be cooked in a smaller slow cooker, such as a 4-quart variety. Everything in this book freezes well, with the exception of the fresh salsas.

Prebrowning
Some recipes call for browning or sautéing ingredients before placing them in the slow cooker. This extra step adds color and an extra layer of flavor, but in most cases it can be skipped if you are in a hurry. One exception is charring or toasting chiles (see below), which is necessary to get the desired results.

Chiles
Chiles are primarily used to add flavor—*not* heat—and many famous dishes, such as mole, are not at all spicy. Any step involving fresh or dried chiles, such as roasting, toasting, soaking, pureeing, or frying them, is essential for developing authentic Mexican flavor. These very simple steps will make an enormous difference in the taste, color, and texture of your finished dish and should not be skipped. (If you're concerned about a chile being too spicy, you can knock down the heat factor by simply removing the seeds and ribs.)

Seasoning
Dry toasting whole spices and grinding them just before adding them to the slow cooker will give you a remarkable boost in fragrance and flavor. Long cooking times can dull the taste of spices, so the quantities in these recipes have been increased slightly to compensate. Some salt should be added at the beginning of cooking, but always taste the final dish and adjust the seasoning to your taste before serving.

USING FRESH CHILES

Fresh chiles are usually charred or roasted before being adding to these recipes.

To roast larger chiles, turn on a gas burner and set the whole chiles directly in the flame, turning occasionally, until evenly blistered and lightly charred on all sides. Alternatively, the chiles can be charred beneath a hot broiler. Wrap the charred chiles in paper towels until cool, then remove the stem, split open, and remove the seeds. Rub off the charred skin with your fingers and use the chiles as directed.

To roast smaller fresh chiles, line the bottom of a heavy skillet with aluminum foil and place over high heat. Place the whole chiles in the pan (without oil) and roast on all sides until blistered, turning occasionally.

The following are the fresh chiles most commonly used in Mexican cooking, listed from the mildest to the hottest.

Bell peppers. Diced bell peppers, usually red or green but also available in yellow, orange, or purple, can either be sautéed or added raw.

Fresno. Small, pointed, and bright red, fresno chiles (sometimes called lipstick peppers) are mild and sweet with thin flesh. They are usually used raw, but may be roasted or stuffed.

Anaheim. Also known as California or chilaca chiles, these large but narrow pale green chiles have a mild flavor but a true chile taste. They must be charred, peeled, and seeded before use. When dried, they are called guajillo chiles.

Poblano. These large, shiny, dark green chiles have a rich, almost smoky flavor. They may be spicy, and they must be charred, peeled, and seeded before use. When dried, they are known as ancho or pasilla chiles.

New Mexico green. Similar in shape to an Anaheim chile, these are darker in color and predictably spicy. They must be charred, peeled, and seeded before use.

Jalapeño. Small, plump, and shiny green, sometimes with red patches, jalapeños may be minced (with or without their seeds) and added raw to fresh salsas. Roasted and seeded, they may be used in salsas or cut into *rajas* (strips). When ripe, dried, and smoked, they are known as chipotles.

Güero. Pale yellow with a waxy sheen, güero chiles pack a spicy punch. They may be used raw in salsas, but are more often roasted and eaten whole or stuffed.

Serrano. Small, dark green, and slender, serranos are hotter than jalapeños. Usually minced (with or without their seeds), they are often added raw to fresh salsas.

Habanero. This small, bright orange chile has a pervasive burning heat that makes the lips tingle.

USING DRIED CHILES

The flavor of dried chiles is developed by toasting them over direct heat, and it blossoms into its full complexity when the chiles are soaked in a little water. Once soft, the chiles can be pureed and worked into the recipe by simmering with other ingredients or frying to intensify the flavor.

To toast dried chiles, stem, split, and seed the chiles and remove any ribs. Heat a heavy cast-iron skillet over medium-high heat. Add the chiles to the dry pan and press down firmly with a spatula until the chiles blister, soften, and darken, being careful not to burn them. Turn the chiles and repeat. Transfer the chiles to a bowl and pour hot water over them as directed in the recipe. Once they have soaked for the time indicated, transfer the soaked chiles to a blender and puree with the reserved soaking liquid, according to the recipe instructions. Puree the chiles for several minutes, until perfectly smooth, scraping down the sides of the blender once or twice. At this point, you can pass the pureed chiles through a food mill to remove any traces of skin or fiber from the sauce, if you like. The chile puree may now be added to the slow cooker, or it may be cooked in a skillet to thicken it and concentrate the flavors.

The following are the dried chiles most commonly used in Mexican cooking, listed from the mildest to the hottest.

Ancho. Deep flavors of fruit, hay, tobacco, and chocolate characterize this wide chile, 3 to 4 inches in length, with wrinkled skin that is reddish-black to black.

Chile negro. Similar in flavor to the ancho chile, this long, narrow chile has smooth, thin flesh that is dark brown to black in color.

Guajillo (mild or spicy). The most commonly used dried chile in Mexican cooking, narrow guajillos are 4 to 6 inches in length and have smooth reddish to dark red skin and leathery flesh. This sweet-smelling chile, often used in enchilada sauce, has a pure chile flavor.

New Mexico. Similar in appearance to the guajillo, this chile may be dark red to red-brown and usually has medium-spicy leathery flesh. Not sweet, this herbaceous chile features the flavors of hay and tobacco.

Puya. Narrow and 3 to 4 inches in length, this red, smooth-skinned chile, also known as a japonés chile, is medium-hot, with a fruity taste.

Chipotle. A smoked dried jalapeño chile, a chipotle is light to medium brown with dry-looking skin. It is smoky, slightly bitter, and very spicy.

Chile de árbol. A small, thin red chile with many seeds, this is hot, with a bitter edge.

Pequín. This tiny red chile is very hot.

Liquids

Slow cooking coaxes the juices out of the food and intensifies natural flavors, so don't be tempted to add too much liquid to your slow cooker. If necessary, you can always thin a well-flavored sauce at the end of cooking, which is better than drowning your food in a watery sauce.

Timing

Meat will cook faster than vegetables in a slow cooker, so arrange hard vegetables on the bottom and around the sides of the slow cooker insert. Cut vegetables in cubes of about $1/2$ inch so they cook evenly. Root vegetables—carrots, potatoes, and the like—must be peeled.

Cooking times may vary slightly depending on the brand of your cooker. The food is done when the meats are very tender and the food smells wonderful. If you want something to cook faster, preheat the cooker and use hot ingredients, like browned meats and hot stocks. If you want something to cook more slowly, start with cold ingredients. And, though it might sound like odd advice in a book on slow cookers, don't overcook the food. Longer is not necessarily better. A slow cooker with a digital timer and an automatic warm cycle (see page 4) will ensure that your lovely *guisado* doesn't cook to mush while you are away.

Low versus High Setting

Long, slow cooking works magic on food, so nearly all of the recipes in this book are cooked on the low setting. Slower cooking allows flavors to develop, sauces to thicken, and meats to become meltingly tender. Foods cooked on high might be done more quickly, but they also might taste watery and boiled.

Stirring

After the ingredients start to simmer, it is perfectly okay to stir the food occasionally; the cooking time should not be affected.

Dealing with a Noisy Lid

If the lid of your slow cooker clatters while it simmers, slip a small piece of folded paper towel under one edge of the lid.

Storing and Reheating Leftovers

Slow cooker food tastes even better the next day, and once a dish is chilled overnight, it's easy to remove any excess fat, which floats to the surface.

Chill leftover food as soon as possible. Remove the food from the slow cooker insert as soon as it is done and spread it in a thin layer on a rimmed baking sheet until cool enough to refrigerate. (*Caldos* and soups should be transferred to smaller containers and either immersed in ice or stirred until cooled.) Next, thoroughly chill the food *uncovered* to minimize crystallization, then freeze. I fill quart- and gallon-sized zippered freezer bags with the food, date them, and freeze them flat. The food freezes quickly, stores neatly, and thaws in a hurry.

Thawing is best done overnight in the refrigerator. To reheat, place the thawed food in a pot or pan, bring to a high simmer or boil, and cook, stirring, for at least 5 minutes. Never thaw or reheat food in the slow cooker.

Other Essential Kitchen Tools

Having the right tools makes cooking easier. For an efficient kitchen, try to purchase fewer, smaller, and more versatile tools. Call me old-fashioned, but simple is often best.

BLENDER. A basic 2-quart blender with simple settings is all you need. I prefer one with a narrow-bottomed jar, which makes it more efficient for blending small amounts.

COMAL OR GRIDDLE. A heavy cast-iron griddle, known as a *comal* in Mexico, is useful when making these dishes, but if you have limited space, a large cast-iron skillet works just as well for toasting ingredients and cooking and warming tortillas. Nonstick griddles are not suitable for high-heat cooking.

CUTTING BOARDS. Buy wood or plastic cutting boards that are generously sized. Use one for vegetables and a separate one for raw meat or chicken. Wash and sanitize cutting boards immediately after using them.

FOOD MILL. A plastic or metal food mill (I like the Moulinex brand) sits over a bowl and quickly cranks out velvety moles and salsas. It can also be used to make fluffy mashed potatoes, creamy purees, and perfect sauces.

FOOD PROCESSOR. A processor with a 2-quart bowl and on, off, and pulse switches is all you need.

KITCHEN TIMER. A small digital timer with a large display is always useful. Mine, which clips to my apron, helps me stay on track when I have many jobs going on at once.

KNIVES. You will spend a lot of time with your knives over a lifetime of cooking, so I recommend that you buy at least one top-quality knife, preferably an 8- or 10-inch French-style chef's knife, and a good sharpening steel. Have your knives professionally sharpened every 6 months and use the steel before each use. A couple of inexpensive paring knives and a serrated knife are all you need to complete your set.

PANS. For high-heat cooking, such as dry roasting or browning, you can't beat well-seasoned cast-iron skillets. They never warp or break or lose their handles, and, if you treat them right, they will last at least a couple of lifetimes. I buy mine for a few dollars apiece at yard sales or swap meets and reseason them myself. If you buy new pans, buy the heaviest ones you can find. Nonstick pans are not suitable for high heat cooking.

SIEVES. Inexpensives sieves are useful for rinsing, straining, and sifting. A 4-inch nylon or metal fine-mesh sieve and an 8-inch metal coarse-mesh should be all you need.

SLOW COOKER. The ideal slow cooker should have low, high, and warm settings and a digital timer. A moderately priced cooker with these features works just as well as a high-end one. If you plan to use the slow cooker a lot, buy a few in different sizes.

SPICE GRINDER. An inexpensive coffee grinder should be reserved for grinding spices only. Wipe it out with a paper towel after each use.

UTENSILS. Metal tools will scratch the earthenware insert of your slow cooker. Silicone and wooden spatulas and spoons, on the other hand, won't scratch your cooker and don't get too hot (ow!). Metal tongs are always handy for handling hot foods, turning chiles or meat in a frying pan, or transferring chiles from the soaking liquid to the blender. I often use simple wooden chopsticks for handling food, and they can double as a rack in the bottom of an oval slow cooker.

KITCHEN TECHNIQUE BASICS

Brown: To cook over medium to high heat in a small amount of fat until deep-brown. Don't stir or move the food until the brown crust has developed.

Dice: To cut into neat, evenly sized cubes.

Fry: To cook until golden in $1/4$ inch to $1/2$ inch hot fat.

Simmer: To cook just below a boil.

Sauté: To cook food quickly over high heat, stirring to cook evenly.

Puree: To blend (in a blender, not a food processor) with a very small amount of liquid until thick and smooth, which may take several minutes. Scrape down the sides of the blender several times. For a perfectly smooth puree, run the puree through a food mill.

Soups

Sopa de Frijol • 13
SPICY BEEF SOUP WITH MAYOCOBA BEANS

Sopa Azteca • 15
CHICKEN SOUP WITH TORTILLAS AND AVOCADO

Puchero de Res • 16
BEEF SOUP WITH CORN AND POTATOES

Menudo • 18
TRIPE SOUP

Pozole Rojo • 19
JALISCO-STYLE RED POZOLE WITH PORK

Pozole Verde • 21
GREEN POZOLE WITH CHICKEN

Menestra, or Sopa de Verduras • 22
MARKET VEGETABLE SOUP

Sopa de Albondigas Verdes • 23
HERBED MEATBALLS IN BEEF SOUP

Mole de Olla con Bolitas • 24
BEEF SOUP WITH CHILE, VEGETABLES,
AND DUMPLINGS

Sopa de Lentejas y Longaniza • 25
LENTIL SOUP WITH LONGANIZA SAUSAGE

Sopa de Fideos • 26
TOMATO SOUP WITH CAPELLINI, AVOCADO,
AND CHICHARRÓN

Sopa de Habas • 27
DRIED FAVA BEAN SOUP WITH FRESH TOMATO
AND GARLIC

Sopa de Elote y Calabaza • 28
FRESH CORN AND ZUCCHINI SOUP

Chileatole • 30
GREEN CHILE SOUP WITH CORN

Sopa de Queso • 31
CHEESE SOUP WITH GREEN CHILE AND POTATO

Consommé de Camarón • 32
SINALOAN DRIED SHRIMP BROTH

Caldo de Camarones • 33
SHRIMP SOUP WITH VEGETABLES

Using just a handful of simple ingredients, Mexican cooks excel at creating soulful, delicious soups out of what seems like nothing. Simple *caldo* (what we call stock or broth) is the base of most Mexican soups, as well as a flavorful addition to many sauces, moles, and stews.

Most Mexican kitchens have a pot of some type of *caldo* bubbling away on the stove, tossed together from bits of chicken or beef and a few vegetables and herbs. *Caldos* are easy to make in the slow cooker—easier than on the stove top, really—and require no attention.

Add more vegetables, meat, chiles, and spices to the broth to create a substantial soup for the midday or evening meal, like Sopa Azteca (page 15) or Puchero de Res (page 16). Caldo de mariscos (seafood soup) is a coastal soup with many variations, like Caldo de Camarones (page 33), which is full of fresh shrimp.

Hearty *ollas* and *pucheros,* also based on a *caldo,* are brothy stews that are full of meat, usually vegetables, and a starch such as potato. Some, like Mole de Olla con Bolitas (page 24) and Pozole Rojo (page 19) and Pozole Verde (page 21), reach far back into pre-Spanish culinary traditions. They are usually rich with dried chiles and *nixtmal* (hominy) or thickened with ground nuts and herbs.

Purely indigenous *atoles,* which predate the arrival of the Spanish in Mexico, can be either a soup or a drink. Based on water thickened with dried or fresh corn or nuts, they are seasoned with chiles and herbs and ground to a smooth consistency. Authentic Aztec *xocolatl* (chocolate drink) is an *atole* made of cocoa beans ground with nuts and chiles and thickened with corn. Bright-green Chileatole (page 30) is made of fresh corn and poblano chiles.

Sopa seca is peasant food: simple and quick to make, it is also, more importantly, filling and cheap. These are made by pouring a boiling liquid (either *caldo,* boiled and sieved tomatoes, or water) over fried pasta, rice, or slices of bread and simmering until the starch absorbs most of the liquid and forms a nearly dry soup. This is old-fashioned home cooking, Mexican style.

Sopa de Frijol

SPICY BEEF SOUP WITH MAYOCOBA BEANS ↓ Serves 4 to 6

Northern Mexican cooks make an art of simple cowboy cooking with this substantial soup with a *picante* kick—just the thing for a cold night. The yellow-green mayocoba beans (also known as peruviana) cook with the beef, absorbing the rich chipotle-infused broth until they are pale and creamy-soft. Any pink, red, or brown bean, such as pinto, bayo, or flor de mayo, may be substituted. This soup has a definite kick. If you prefer a milder version, you can reduce or omit the chipotles.

2 large poblano chiles
1 cup dried mayocoba beans, rinsed and picked over
2 jalapeño chiles, stemmed and cut lengthwise into strips
2$^1/_2$ pounds very lean chuck or stew beef, cut into $^3/_4$-inch cubes
4 slices bacon
1 large white onion, diced
4 large cloves garlic, minced
1 tablespoon kosher salt
1 tablespoon whole cumin seeds
1 tablespoon dried epazote or whole dried Mexican oregano
1 (7-ounce) can chipotles in adobo, with liquid, finely chopped
1 (14-ounce) can diced tomatoes in juice, or 3 Roma tomatoes, finely chopped
4 cups Caldo de Res (page 96), or more as needed
2 cups water

TO SERVE
Warm corn or flour tortillas

Char the poblanos over a gas flame or under a broiler until they are blistered on all sides. Let cool slightly, then peel, seed, and cut into 1-inch pieces.

Place the beans in the bottom of a 5-quart slow cooker. Top with the poblanos, jalapeños, beef, bacon, onion, garlic, salt, cumin, and epazote. Add the chipotles, tomatoes, broth, and water to the cooker. Cover and cook on low for 8 hours.

Turn the cooker to the warm setting and uncover. Let the soup settle for 15 minutes, then, using a large spoon, skim off as much fat as possible. Remove the bacon, cut it into small pieces, and return to the soup. Thin the soup, if desired, with a little more broth or water. Taste and adjust the seasoning. Serve hot with warm corn or flour tortillas on the side.

VARIATIONS
- Substitute cubes of peeled red or white rose potato for the beans.
- For smoky flavor without the heat, substitute 3 tablespoons soy bacon bits for the chipotles.

Sopa Azteca

CHICKEN SOUP WITH TORTILLAS AND AVOCADO ↙ Serves 4 to 6

There are as many recipes for this soup as there are cooks in Mexico. One of the simplest versions consists only of a bit of sautéed tomato and water poured over lightly fried corn tortillas. This flavorful version gets its zip from tomatillos, dried chiles, and fresh herbs.

2 guajillo chiles, stemmed and seeded
1/2 cup hot water
2 tomatillos, husked and washed
2 Roma tomatoes
1/2 small white onion, diced
1 large clove garlic
1 small carrot, peeled and finely diced
2 chicken breasts (about 1 1/2 pounds total)
2 teaspoons kosher salt
5 cups Caldo de Pollo (page 95)
2 cups water
1/4 cup fresh cilantro leaves, or 12 fresh
  epazote leaves, shredded

TO SERVE
3 corn tortillas
2 tablespoons vegetable oil
Diced Hass avocado
Lime wedges

Heat a heavy skillet over medium-high heat. Add the chiles and toast on both sides, turning occasionally and pressing down with a spatula, until they soften and blister. Remove from the pan. When the chiles are cool enough to handle, tear them into small pieces and place in a heatproof bowl. Add the hot water and soak the chiles, stirring occasionally, for 30 minutes.

While the chiles soak, line the skillet with a piece of aluminum foil. Add the tomatillos to the skillet and roast over medium-high heat, turning occasionally, until lightly charred in spots and softened. Remove the tomatillos from the skillet.

In a blender, combine the chiles and their soaking liquid, the tomatillos, tomatoes, onion, and garlic and puree until very smooth. (For a smoother texture, you can press the mixture through a fine-mesh sieve, if you like.) Transfer the puree to a 5-quart slow cooker. Add the carrot, chicken, salt, broth, and water and stir. Cover and cook on low for 4 hours, or until the chicken is tender.

While the chicken is cooking, cut the tortillas in half, then cut the halves into strips 1/4 inch wide (or cut them into small squares.) Heat the oil in a small skillet and fry the tortillas until crisp. Drain on paper towels.

Remove the chicken from the slow cooker and discard the skin and bones. Shred or dice the chicken into 1-inch pieces and return to the broth. Add the cilantro. Heat through, taste, and adjust the seasoning.

To serve, divide the fried tortilla pieces among the serving bowls and ladle the hot soup over them, including some of the chicken in each bowl. Garnish with a few pieces of avocado and serve very hot with the lime wedges on the side.

VARIATIONS
- Scatter a bit of grated Monterey jack cheese or queso fresco over the tortillas before you pour the hot soup on top.
- Add 1 cup cooked garbanzo beans to the cooker for the last hour of cooking.

Puchero de Res

BEEF SOUP WITH CORN AND POTATOES ⤓ Serves 4 to 6

Hearty *puchero de res* is a classic home-style soup that is served in every tiny *lonchería* (a snack bar usually run by a one woman who cooks and serves) and *fonda* (an inexpensive home-style restaurant) in Mexico. It always includes generous chunks of beef and corn, plus potato or yam and the cook's choice of seasonal vegetables. It's one of easiest soups to make: just toss everything in the cooker, turn it on low, and let the magic happen. Note that the jalapeño is not stemmed; that keeps the seeds from falling out and floating around the soup. The soup may become quite thick when cooked, so you may want to add more broth at the end. Presented in big bowls with the tortillas on the side, there isn't much more you could want.

2 Roma tomatoes, roasted (see page 133)
4 cloves garlic, peeled
1 large poblano chile, stemmed, seeded, and diced
1 white onion, diced
2 small carrots, peeled and sliced
1 ear fresh corn, husked and cut into 6 (1-inch) wheels
1 jalapeño chile, split in half lengthwise
1 small white rose potato or yam, peeled and cut into 1-inch cubes
1 small zucchini, such as green calabaza or chayote, cut into 1-inch cubes
1 tablespoon kosher salt
1 teaspoon freshly ground black pepper
2 pounds lean stew beef, cut into 1-inch cubes
5 cups Caldo de Res (page 96), or more as needed
2 cups water

TO SERVE
Warm corn tortillas

In a blender, combine the roasted tomato and garlic and puree until smooth. Transfer the puree to a 6-quart slow cooker and add all the remaining ingredients, placing the harder vegetables on the bottom and the meat on top. Cover and cook on low for 8 hours.

Turn the cooker to the warm setting and uncover. Let the soup settle for 15 minutes, then, using a large spoon, skim off as much fat as possible. Taste and adjust the seasoning. Serve in big bowls, with the tortillas on the side.

VARIATION
• Add 1 cup cooked garbanzo beans during the last hour of cooking.

Menudo

TRIPE SOUP ⟱ Serves 8

Menudo is considered a surefire cure for just about anything from a hangover to a broken heart. It's true: the world *does* look sunnier over a huge bowl of steaming menudo with all the garnishes and a cold beer. Though I am not generally a fan of tripe, I adore menudo's unique flavor and rich, gelatinous broth (not to mention its miraculous restorative powers). You may use either honeycomb tripe or the more delicate "book" tripe in this dish, but be sure it is already well cleaned when you buy it. Hunting down the unusual ingredients can be time-consuming, so this recipe makes enough for eight servings—plenty to enjoy now and freeze for later.

6 guajillo chiles, stemmed and seeded
1 cup hot water
1 pound tripe, rinsed
1 (28-ounce) can hominy and its liquid
1 calf's foot, split (see Note)
1 head garlic, split into cloves
1 white onion, peeled and cut into wide strips
1 tablespoon kosher salt
1 tablespoon whole black peppercorns
1 dried bay leaf
1 tablespoon whole coriander seed
8 to 10 cups Caldo de Res (page 96) or water

TO SERVE
Warm corn tortillas
Whole dried Mexican oregano
Lime wedges
Ground hot pequín chile or crushed red chiles
Sliced radishes
Diced white onion
Chopped fresh cilantro

Heat a heavy skillet over medium-high heat. Add the chiles and toast on both sides, turning occasionally and pressing down with a spatula, until they soften and blister. Remove from the pan. When the chiles are cool enough to handle, tear them into small pieces and place in a heatproof bowl. Add the hot water and soak the chiles, stirring occasionally, for 30 minutes.

Transfer the chiles with their soaking liquid to a blender and puree until very smooth. (For a smoother texture, you can press the puree through a fine-mesh sieve, if you like.) Transfer the puree to 6-quart slow cooker.

Rinse the tripe and cut into 1-inch pieces. Add to slow cooker along with the hominy, calf's foot, garlic, onion, salt, peppercorns, bay leaf, coriander, and broth.

Cover and cook on low for 8 hours. Remove the calf's foot. When it's cool enough to handle, pick off any bits of meat and return them to the pot, discarding all the bones and skin. Taste the soup and adjust the seasoning. Serve very hot in large bowls, with warm tortillas on the side and small bowls of the garnishes on the table.

NOTE
If you like, you can substitute 2 pounds of sawn beef shin bones for the calf's foot.

Pozole Rojo

JALISCO-STYLE RED POZOLE WITH PORK ↓ *Serves 4 to 6*

A good pozole is primarily about the *nixtamal* (hominy), which blossoms while it cooks with the pork and chiles and adds wonderful flavor to the broth. Like almost everything made with corn, pozole has ancient roots in Mexico and many regional variations. This version, made with mild dried red chiles, is a favorite at fiestas and family gatherings. Serve the pozole in very large bowls, with the traditional garnishes in small dishes on the table for all to share.

4 large guajillo or New Mexico chiles,
   stemmed and seeded
1/2 cup hot water
1 head garlic, washed and halved horizontally
1 white onion, peeled and halved with root
   end intact
2 teaspoons whole cumin seeds
2 teaspoons whole dried Mexican oregano
1 tablespoon kosher salt
1 (28-ounce) can white hominy with liquid
2 pounds meaty pork neck bones
1 pound boneless pork shoulder, cut into
   4 pieces
1 pig's foot, split
5 cups Caldo de Res (page 96) or Caldo de Pollo
   (page 95)
4 1/2 cups water

TO SERVE
Warm corn tortillas
Lime wedges
Whole dried Mexican oregano
Sliced radishes
Diced white onion
Bottled hot sauce or ground hot pequín chile
Shredded lettuce or green cabbage

Heat a heavy skillet over medium-high heat. Add the chiles and toast on both sides, turning occasionally and pressing down with a spatula, until they soften and blister. Remove from the pan.

When the chiles are cool enough to handle, tear them into small pieces and place in a heatproof bowl. Add the hot water and soak the chiles, stirring occasionally, for 30 minutes.

In a blender, puree the chiles with their soaking liquid until perfectly smooth. (For a smoother texture, you can press the mixture through a fine-mesh sieve, if you like.) Transfer the puree to a 6-quart slow cooker.

Add the garlic, onion, cumin seeds, oregano, and salt, and then add the hominy, pork neck bones, pork shoulder, pig's foot, broth, and water. Cover and cook on low for 8 hours, or until the meat is tender. Do not stir after the first 2 hours.

Turn the cooker to the warm setting and uncover. Let the soup settle for 15 minutes. With a kitchen spoon, skim off any excess fat that rises to the surface. Remove and discard the garlic and onion. Using a slotted spoon, carefully lift the meats onto a plate, keeping them as intact as possible. Discard the pig's foot. Carefully remove any small bones from the soup. Break the pork shoulder into chunks and return to the cooker. Shred the meat from the neck bones and return to the cooker. Taste and adjust the seasoning.

Serve with the garnishes at the table.

Pozole Verde

GREEN POZOLE WITH CHICKEN ↙ *Serves 4 to 6*

This sumptuous pale-green pozole is thickened with a classic and thoroughly authentic salsa of green tomatillos and ground pumpkin seeds, spicy with green chiles and bursting with the fresh flavor of cilantro. Frying the salsa before adding it to the soup brings out its remarkable flavor. Garnishes of crunchy *chicharrón* (fried pork skin) and creamy avocado make this chicken pozole truly festive.

2 chicken breasts
1 head garlic, washed and halved horizontally
1 white onion, peeled and halved, with root
 end intact
1 tablespoon kosher salt
1 tablespoon whole cumin seeds
1 (28-ounce) can white hominy and liquid
4 cups Caldo de Pollo (page 95)
5 cups water
4 sprigs fresh epazote, or 6 sprigs fresh cilantro

SALSA VERDE
1/2 cup raw pepitas (pumpkin seeds)
6 to 8 tomatillos (1/2 pound), husked and washed
1 cup diced white onion
1 clove garlic, peeled
2 serrano chiles, stemmed
1 bunch fresh cilantro, leaves and small stems,
 coarsely chopped (about 1 cup packed)
2 teaspoons fresh lard or vegetable oil

TO SERVE
Diced white onion
Minced serrano chile
Lime wedges
Crumbled chicharrón
Diced Hass avocado

In a 6-quart slow cooker, combine the chicken, garlic, onion, salt, cumin seeds, hominy, broth, and water. Cover and cook on low for 4 hours, until the chicken is tender and cooked through but not falling apart. Remove the chicken and let cool. Discard the chicken bones and skin and break the meat into large pieces. Refrigerate the meat until needed. Add the epazote and continue cooking the soup on low (without the chicken) for 2 hours more.

While the soup is cooking, make the salsa. Heat a 10-inch sauté pan over medium heat. Toast the pepitas in the dry pan, stirring often, until crunchy and olive-green. Let cool completely.

Place the tomatillos in a small pot and cover with cold water. Bring to a simmer over medium-high heat and simmer for 5 minutes, or just until tender. Drain and place in a blender along with the cooled pepitas, onion, garlic, serranos, and cilantro. Add 1/2 cup broth from the slow cooker and puree, scraping down the sides several times, until very smooth, about 2 minutes. (For a smoother texture, you can press the mixture through a fine-mesh sieve if you like.)

Heat the sauté pan over medium heat. Add the lard, then pour in the contents of the blender. Cook, stirring often, until the sauce is thickened and pale green, 5 to 7 minutes. If the sauce splatters, reduce the heat.

To finish the soup, discard the onion, garlic, and epazote. Stir the salsa into the hot soup. Add the chicken to the soup and cook on low for 30 minutes. Taste and adjust the seasoning. Serve in large bowls, with the garnishes alongside.

Menestra, or Sopa de Verduras

MARKET VEGETABLE SOUP ⤓ *Serves 4 to 6*

Several times each week, mobile street markets called *tianguis* bring beautiful seasonal vegetables (and just about everything else) to Mexican neighborhoods. Inspired by those markets, this simple soup is easy to put together using any vegetables you have on hand—or you can choose whatever catches your fancy at the farmers' market. Bring out all the flavor with a final garnish of fried corn tortillas, crumbled guajillo chiles, and cotija cheese.

1 poblano chile, roasted (see page 5), seeded, and diced

1/2 cup dried garbanzo beans

1 small leek, trimmed of dark green leaves, cleaned, quartered, and sliced

1 small white onion, diced

1/2 small carrot, peeled and finely diced

2 cloves garlic, minced

1/2 cup fresh corn kernels

2 cups finely diced mixed seasonal vegetables, such as zucchini, green beans, red bell pepper, yams, green cabbage, green beans, white mushrooms, peas, or kale

1 (14-ounce) can diced tomatoes in juice, or 3 ripe tomatoes, diced

2 dried bay leaves

1 tablespoon kosher salt

1 teaspoon freshly ground black pepper

1/2 teaspoon dried thyme

8 cups water, or more as needed

TO SERVE

2 guajillo chiles, stemmed and seeded

1 tablespoon vegetable oil

2 corn tortillas

2 ounces crumbled cotija cheese (optional)

Combine all the soup ingredients in a 5-quart slow cooker, cover, and cook on low for 7 hours, checking occasionally and adding more water if needed. Taste and adjust the seasoning.

While the soup cooks, make the garnishes. Heat a heavy skillet over medium-high heat. Add the chiles and toast on both sides, turning occasionally and pressing down with a spatula, until dry and quite dark, but not burned. Remove from the pan. When the chiles are cool enough to handle, crumble into small pieces.

In the same skillet, heat the oil over medium heat. Cut the tortillas into 1/2-inch squares and fry until crisp. Drain on a paper towel.

Serve the soup very hot, garnished with some of the fried tortilla squares, a sprinkle of crumbled chiles, and some cotija cheese, if desired.

Sopa de Albondigas Verdes

HERBED MEATBALLS IN BEEF SOUP ⤲ Serves 4 to 6

Sopa de albondigas is simple to make, especially if you have a batch of beef broth simmering away in your slow cooker. Here, the meatballs are seasoned with cilantro, oregano, and a bit of spicy green serrano chile. Squeeze a wedge of lime over the soup at the table to wake up all the flavors.

3/4 pound ground pork
3/4 pound ground beef
2 large eggs, beaten
1/4 cup fresh white bread crumbs
2 tablespoons minced garlic
1 teaspoon whole dried Mexican oregano
1 tablespoon kosher salt
1 teaspoon freshly ground black pepper
1 large bunch fresh cilantro, very finely chopped
1 cup diced white onion
2 large serrano chiles, stemmed
6 cups Caldo de Res (page 96)

TO SERVE
Minced fresh flat-leaf parsley
1 Roma tomato, seeded and finely diced
Arroz al Vapor (page 99)
Lime wedges
Crumbled chicharrón (optional)
Diced Hass avocado (optional)

Combine the pork, beef, and eggs in a bowl using your hands. In a food processor, combine the bread crumbs, garlic, oregano, 2 teaspoons of the salt, the pepper, and cilantro and pulse until finely ground. Transfer to the bowl with the meat mixture. Add the onion and serranos to the food processor and pulse until finely minced. Add to the meat mixture and combine thoroughly. With damp hands, divide the meat mixture into 12 or 24 equal portions. Roll into balls and chill for at least 1 hour, or up to overnight.

Place the meatballs in a 5-quart slow cooker. Add the broth and the remaining 1 teaspoon salt. Cover and cook on low until the meatballs are firm and cooked through, about 4 hours.

Serve hot in large bowls, garnished with the parsley and diced tomatoes. Pass the cooked rice on the side and serve with small bowls of lime, *chicharrón*, and diced avocado, on the table.

VARIATIONS
• To cut the calories and fat content, reduce the meats to 1/2 cup each and add 1/2 cup cooked rice to the albondigas mixture.

• Substitute an equal amount of ground turkey for the ground beef, the ground pork, or both.

Mole de Olla con Bolitas

BEEF SOUP WITH CHILE, VEGETABLES, AND DUMPLINGS ⨼ Serves 4 to 6

This mole is not a thick sauce but a classic Mexican soup, aromatic with dried chiles and epazote and loaded with chunks of meat and vegetables. A proper *mole de olla* always includes pieces of fresh corn and *ejotes* (green beans). This version also includes delicious little masa dumplings called *bolitas*.

4 ancho chiles, stemmed and seeded
1 cup hot water
6 tomatillos, husked and washed
$1/2$ white onion, diced
2 cloves garlic
2 teaspoons vegetable oil
$1^1/2$ pounds lean stew beef, cut into 1-inch cubes
7 cups water
2 kosher teaspoons salt
2 teaspoons whole cumin seeds
4 ounces green beans, cut into 1-inch pieces (about 1 cup)
1 zucchini, cut into 1-inch pieces (about $1^1/2$ cups)
1 ear fresh corn, husked and cut into 6 (1-inch) wheels
12 fresh epazote leaves

TO SERVE
Bolitas (recipe follows)
Hass avocado wedges
Warm corn tortillas

Heat a heavy skillet over medium-high heat. Add the chiles and toast on both sides, turning occasionally and pressing down with a spatula, until they soften and blister. Remove from the pan. When the chiles are cool enough to handle, tear them into small pieces and place in a heatproof bowl. Add the hot water and soak the chiles, stirring occasionally, for 30 minutes.

While the chiles are soaking, place the tomatillos in a small saucepan, cover with water, and simmer for 5 minutes, or just until tender. Drain.

In a blender, combine the chiles and their soaking liquid, tomatillos, onion, and garlic and puree until very smooth. (For a smoother texture, you can press the mixture through a fine-mesh sieve, if you like.)

Heat the oil in a 10-inch skillet. Add the puree and cook, stirring, until the sauce is thickened and fragrant, about 5 minutes. Transfer to a 5-quart slow cooker along with the beef, water, salt, cumin, green beans, zucchini, and corn. Cover and cook on low for 6 hours.

When the soup is almost ready, make the *bolitas* (see opposite). About 15 minutes before you're ready to serve the soup, add the epazote and *bolitas,* cover, and cook until the *bolitas* float to the surface, about 15 minutes. Serve hot with wedges of avocado and warm tortillas.

Bolitas

¼ cup milk
1 tablespoon butter, melted
1 large egg
1 teaspoon kosher salt
About ⅓ cup dry masa harina (preferably
   Maseca brand)

In a bowl, combine the milk and butter. Stir in the egg and salt until thoroughly combined. With a fork, stir in the masa harina to form a dough that is soft but not sticky. With damp hands, form small teaspoonfuls of the masa into balls. Flatten each ball slightly, and indent lightly on both sides with your thumb and forefinger. Drop into the simmering soup. When they float, they are done.

VARIATION

- Instead of making bolitas, about 30 minutes before you're ready to serve the soup, ladle 1 cup hot soup from the slow cooker into a bowl and stir in ¼ cup dry masa harina. When the mixture is well blended, whisk into the soup and cook another 30 minutes.

Sopa de Lentejas y Longaniza

LENTIL SOUP WITH LONGANIZA SAUSAGE ☙ Serves 4 to 6

Mexican *carnicerías* (butchers) sell long, looping skeins of *longaniza,* a mild pork sausage flavored with garlic, red chile, cumin, and oregano (not to be confused with the Spanish or Filipino sausages of the same name, which are very different). *Longaniza* is widely used in Mexican cooking, though it is less well known in the United States. A quality Mexican pork chorizo may be substituted. This high-fiber soup, packed with vegetables, freezes well.

10 ounces cured (firm) Mexican longaniza
1 white onion, finely diced
1 small celery stalk, diced
2 Anaheim chiles, or 1 green bell pepper,
   stemmed, seeded, and diced
1 small carrot, peeled and finely diced
1 small white rose potato, peeled and diced
2 dried bay leaves
1 tablespoon whole dried Mexican oregano
1 tablespoon kosher salt
2¼ cups green lentils (about 1 pound),
   rinsed and picked over
1 (14-ounce) can diced tomatoes in juice
2 guajillo chiles, stemmed and seeded
10 cups water, or more as needed

Remove the casing from the *longaniza* and crumble the sausage into a 6-quart slow cooker. Layer the rest of the remaining ingredients in the slow cooker, in the order that they are listed. Cover and cook on low for 10 hours, checking occasionally and adding more water if needed. Taste and adjust the seasoning before serving hot.

VARIATIONS

- Add 1 small smoked pork hock with the rest of the ingredients.

- To make a vegan soup, substitute ⅓ cup bacon-flavored soy bits for the sausage.

Sopa de Fideos

TOMATO SOUP WITH CAPELLINI, AVOCADO, AND CHICHARRÓN ⤓ Serves 4 to 6

For many, *sopa de fideos* is *the* comforting taste of home. It is served everywhere, every day, in tiny *loncherías*, tony men's clubs, and traditional restaurants as well as at mama's kitchen table. I had this version at the venerable Fonda el Refugio in Mexico City's Zona Rosa, where a crew of formidable female cooks *(las mayoras)* rule the kitchen. This slow cooker recipe takes only a couple of hours from start to finish. It is made with coils of toasted *fideos,* which are similar to capellini, also called angel hair pasta. For the meat, use shredded bits from Caldo de Res (page 96), Shredded Beef (page 97), or any other leftover meat.

4 whole Roma tomatoes
3 cups water
1 (8-ounce) can diced tomatoes in juice
1 1/2 tablespoons vegetable oil
1 (6-ounce) package dried fideos or angel hair pasta
1/2 white onion, diced
1 clove garlic, minced
4 cups Caldo de Pollo (page 95)
1 cup (about 6 ounces) cooked meat, finely diced

TO SERVE
Diced Hass avocado
Crumbled chicharrón
New Mexico or puya chiles, toasted and
    crumbled (see page 6)

Combine the Roma tomatoes and water in a small saucepan. Bring to simmer over medium-high and simmer the tomatoes until softened, about 5 minutes. Drain, reserving the cooking water, and place the tomatoes in a blender along with the canned tomatoes and their juice; don't blend yet.

Heat 1 tablespoon of the oil in a 10-inch skillet over medium heat. Break the *fideos* up into 1-inch pieces and fry slowly, stirring often, until golden brown, about 5 minutes. Remove them from the skillet and drain on a paper towel.

Wipe out the pan and add the remaining 1/2 tablespoon of oil. Sauté the onion and garlic over medium heat stirring often, until soft and golden. Add the onions and garlic to the tomatoes in the blender and puree until very smooth. (For a smoother texture, you can press the puree through a fine-mesh sieve or food mill, if you like.)

Pour the puree back into the hot skillet and fry over medium heat, stirring often, until slightly thickened, about 5 minutes. (If the sauce splatters, reduce the heat.)

Add the puree to the slow cooker along with the broth and reserved tomato cooking liquid. Cover and cook on high for 1 hour, then add the *fideos,* reduce the heat to low, and cook, covered, until the pasta is soft, about 1 hour more. Just before serving, stir in the cooked meat. Serve the soup hot with the avocado, *chicharrón,* and chiles on the side.

VARIATIONS

• To make *sopa seca,* use half the amount of water and caldo. It will be thick, like a soupy pasta. Top with crumbled queso fresco or cotija cheese.

• To make *sopa de tortilla,* do not use fideos. Instead, cut 4 corn tortillas into small squares, fry in vegetable oil until crisp, and divide among the serving bowls. To serve, pour the hot tomato broth over and top each bowl with crumbled queso fresco and a few pieces of diced avocado.

Sopa de Habas

DRIED FAVA BEAN SOUP WITH FRESH TOMATO AND GARLIC ↓ *Serves 4 to 6*

This soup is a typically thrifty and sustaining *sopa de frijol* (bean soup) with the added advantage of being meatless. The *habas*, or dried fava beans, fall apart into tender, skinless crumbs that soak up the other flavors. They have a distinctive taste, but you can also use bayo or pinto beans in this dish. Garnish the soup with your choice of rich, spicy toppings, such as a drizzle of flavorful Baja California olive oil or a sprinkle of spicy chorizo. Ladled over croutons, it becomes a thick, delicious *sopa seca.* Or just enjoy it unadorned to appreciate how flavorful a few simple ingredients can be.

2 cups habas (dried fava beans)
8 cups water
2 teaspoons kosher salt
3 large cloves garlic, peeled
6 whole Roma tomatoes (about 1¹/₂ pounds total)
2 serrano chiles, stemmed
2 tablespoons vegetable oil
1¹/₂ cups diced white onion

OPTIONAL GARNISHES
Extra-virgin olive oil
Freshly ground black pepper
Diced white onions
Chopped fresh cilantro
Fried chorizo
Crumbled chicharrón
Croutons

Rinse and pick over the *habas,* discarding any that are dark. Place in a 4-quart slow cooker with 5 cups of the water, the salt, and 1 of the garlic cloves. Cook on low until the *habas* are falling apart, 4 to 6 hours. Discard the garlic.

Combine the tomatoes and serranos in a small saucepan with the remaining 3 cups of water. Bring to a boil over medium-high heat and boil until softened, about 5 minutes. Drain, reserving the water, and place the tomatoes and serranos in a blender.

Slice the remaining 2 cloves of garlic. Heat 1 tablespoon of the oil in a 10-inch skillet over medium heat. Add the onion and garlic and cook, stirring often, until softened and pale gold, about 5 minutes. Add to the blender with the tomatoes and puree until smooth. (For a smoother texture, you can press the mixture through a fine-mesh sieve, if you like.)

Heat the remaining 1 tablespoon of oil in the same pan over medium heat. Add the tomato puree and cook, stirring often, until thickened, about 10 minutes. Remove from the heat.

Transfer the cooked *habas* and their liquid to the blender. Puree and return to the slow cooker. Add the tomato puree, cover, and reheat on low. Thin the soup as needed with some of the reserved tomato cooking liquid. Taste and adjust the seasoning. Serve as is, or topped with any of the suggested garnishes.

Sopa de Elote y Calabaza

FRESH CORN AND ZUCCHINI SOUP ↙ Serves 4 to 6

This easy soup tastes of the very essence of corn. Try to find sweet yellow corn at your market. It contains more starch than white corn, which naturally thickens the soup, and the long simmering in the slow cooker brings out the corn's natural sweetness. Simmering the scraped cobs with the soup gives it even more flavor, while a final swirl of thick Mexican *crema* gives it a touch of buttery decadence.

4 ears fresh sweet yellow corn
3 tablespoons salted butter
1 white onion, finely diced
1 teaspoon whole coriander seeds, crushed
2 small zucchini or green calabaza squash,
   finely diced (about 2 cups)
6 cups water
1 teaspoon kosher salt
1 tablespoon shredded fresh epazote leaves

TO SERVE
1/3 cup heavy cream or Mexican crema

Remove and discard the husks and silk from the corn and cut the kernels from each cob. You should have about 3 cups of kernels. Reserve the cobs.

In a 10-inch skillet, melt the butter over medium-low heat. Add the onion, corn kernels, and coriander. Cover and cook slowly, stirring occasionally, until the vegetables are softened but not brown, about 5 minutes. Transfer to a 5-quart slow cooker.

Add the corncobs, zucchini, water, and salt to the slow cooker. Cover and cook on low for 6 hours.

Just before serving, remove and discard the corncobs and stir in the epazote. Taste and adjust the seasoning. Ladle the hot soup into bowls and top each with a spoonful of *crema*.

VARIATIONS
- Substitute thinly sliced green onion tops or cilantro for the epazote.
- Sprinkle each serving with ground guajillo or New Mexico chile.

Chileatole

GREEN CHILE SOUP WITH CORN ⤶ Serves 4 to 6

Healthful and sustaining *atoles,* soups and drinks made from corn, are an ancient Mexican tradition. I once had this bright green soup at the Xochimilco market south of Mexico City, where it was paired with a warm cake of fresh ground corn toasted on an earthenware *comal;* it was like tasting Mexico as it was five hundred years ago. This historic area, which is close to the small farms that have fed the city for a thousand years, is a stronghold of traditional pre-Spanish culture and cooking. Despite being vegan and nearly fat-free, *chileatole* is filling and satisfying, so serve it in small portions. Use a light hand with the salt; the soup is mildly sweet from the corn.

1 tablespoon vegetable oil
1 cup diced white onion
2 jalapeño chiles, stemmed, seeded and quartered
4 poblano chiles, roasted (see page 5), seeded and diced
3 Anaheim chiles, roasted (see page 5), seeded and diced
Kernels from 4 ears fresh corn (about 3 cups)
6 cups water, or more as needed
2 teaspoons kosher salt
10 large fresh epazote leaves, shredded (about 2 tablespoons)
1/2 bunch fresh cilantro, finely chopped
1/2 teaspoon freshly ground black pepper

In a 10-inch skillet, heat the oil over medium heat. Add the onion and all the chiles and cook, stirring, until the onion is soft and pale gold, about 5 minutes. Transfer to a 5-quart slow cooker.

Place the corn in a food processor and pulse several times, until the kernels are broken up but it is not quite smooth. Add the corn to the slow cooker along with the water and salt. Cover and cook on low for 6 hours.

Stir in the epazote, cilantro, and pepper. Working in batches, transfer the soup to a blender and puree until velvety smooth, or use an immersion blender to puree the soup in the slow cooker, which will result in a soup with more texture. If necessary, thin the soup with a little water. Taste and adjust the seasoning before serving.

Sopa de Queso

CHEESE SOUP WITH GREEN CHILE AND POTATO ⬇ Serves 4 to 6

Thanks to waves of European immigrants who arrived in the early twentieth century, the northern Mexican state of Chihuahua produces remarkable cheeses. Most are made for export to other parts of the country, but small local dairies still craft young cheeses from raw cows' milk that are never refrigerated. The creamy flavor and melting texture of these old-fashioned cheeses speaks worlds about the goodness of simple country food. This rustic soup is usually made with *menonita* or Chihuahua cheese, which melts with the heat of the broth. Soft Muenster or a mild Gouda is a good substitute.

1 tablespoon salted butter
$^1/_2$ white onion, finely diced
2 cloves garlic, minced
3 Roma tomatoes, finely chopped
1 pound red or white rose potatoes
6 cups Caldo de Res (page 96) or Caldo de Pollo (page 95)
1 teaspoon kosher salt
3 poblano chiles, roasted (see page 5), seeded and diced
10 ounces Chihuahua (menonita) or Muenster cheese, grated

TO SERVE
Chopped fresh cilantro

Heat the butter in a skillet over medium heat. Add the onion and garlic and cook slowly, stirring often, for 2 minutes. Add the tomato and cook, stirring frequently, until the pan is almost dry, about 5 minutes. Transfer to a 5-quart slow cooker.

Peel the potatoes and cut into neat $^1/_2$-inch cubes. You should have about 4 cups. Add to the slow cooker along with the broth and salt. Cover and cook on low for 6 hours. Add the poblanos and cheese and stir slowly until the cheese melts into the soup. Continue cooking on low for 30 minutes more.

To serve, ladle the soup into bowls and sprinkle each serving with a little chopped cilantro.

VARIATIONS

- Roast the tomatoes until they are soft and charred (see page 133) and chop to a pulp before adding to the soup.

- Just before serving, stir in a spoonful of heavy cream or Mexican *crema*.

- Substitute 3 cups of Consommé de Camarón (page 32) plus 3 cups of water, for the beef or chicken broth.

Consommé de Camarón

SINALOAN DRIED SHRIMP BROTH ⬇ Makes 6 servings

In seafood restaurants along the Pacific coast, little cups of hot soup are often served as a free appetizer along with packaged corn tostadas and an array of bottled hot sauces. The rich flavor of this potent broth comes from dried shrimp and plenty of chiles. If diluted, this broth forms an excellent base for Caldo de Camarones (page 33). Serve with a bucket of Pacifico beers on ice.

1 tablespoon vegetable oil
4 guajillo chiles, stemmed and seeded
1 ancho chile, stemmed and seeded
4 to 6 whole chiles de árbol
1/4 cup diced white onion
1 large clove garlic, minced
4 Roma tomatoes, chopped
8 cups water
2 teaspoons kosher salt
2 ounces cleaned dried shrimp (see Note)
2 large sprigs fresh epazote

TO SERVE
Lime wedges
Tostadas

In a 10-inch skillet, heat the oil over medium-high heat. Tear all the chiles into small pieces and add to the skillet, using 4 chiles de árbol for a milder dish, or up to 6 for a spicer one. Cook, stirring, until the chiles begin to color, about 3 minutes. Add the onion, garlic, and tomatoes. Cook, stirring often, until the onion is pale gold and the tomatoes are soft and dry, about 7 minutes. Add 3 cups of the water and simmer until the pan is almost dry, about 15 minutes. Transfer to a blender and puree until smooth.

In a 5-quart slow cooker, combine the puree with the remaining 5 cups water, the salt, and dried shrimp. Cover and cook on low for 4 hours. Add the epazote, cover, and cook 30 minutes more.

To serve, strain the broth and discard the shrimp and epazote. Serve very hot with the lime wedges and tostadas on the side.

NOTE
Dried shrimp are sold in packages, usually with the heads and shells on but sometimes already cleaned. If you buy head-on shrimp, you'll need to buy twice as much and remove the heads and shells before adding them to the soup. I do not recommend using dried ground shrimp.

Caldo de Camarones

SHRIMP SOUP WITH VEGETABLES ⩔ Serves 6

Consommé de Camarón (page 32) forms the base for this quick shrimp soup. If you prefer, the soup can be made with pieces of fish, calamari, clams, mussels, or crab. Or slowly simmer a thick fillet of firm fish such as sea bass in the broth. Instead of the potatoes, you can use brown *fideos* (see Sopa de Fideos, page 26, for the method), or serve the soup with a bowl of cooked rice alongside, which can be added to the soup.

4 cups Consommé de Camarón (page 32)
2 cups water
1/4 cup finely diced carrot
1/4 cup peeled and finely diced white rose or
   red potato
1/4 cup finely diced zucchini
8 ounces medium shrimp, shelled and deveined
   (if desired)

TO SERVE
Lime wedges
Bottled hot sauce

In a soup pot, bring the shrimp broth and water to a simmer. Add the carrot, potato, zucchini, and shrimp and simmer for 15 minutes. At this point, the soup may be transferred to a slow cooker set on warm.

Serve hot with with lime wedges and hot sauce on the side.

Mains and Guisados

Pollo en Crema con Chipotles • 37

CHICKEN AND PEPPERS IN CHIPOTLE CREAM

Pollo en Salsa • 38

CHICKEN IN TOMATO-JALAPEÑO SALSA

Mole Negro • 41

BLACK MOLE

Mole Manchamanteles • 43

RED MOLE WITH CHICKEN AND FRIED PLANTAINS

Costillos • 44

PORK RIBS IN CHIPOTLE-TOMATILLO SALSA

Asado de Bodas • 45

WEDDING STEW WITH PORK

Chile Verde • 47

PORK IN GREEN CHILE SALSA

Carne Pibil • 48

PORK IN BANANA LEAVES WITH ACHIOTE

Albondigas en Salsa Chipotle • 50

MEATBALLS IN CHIPOTLE SAUCE

Carne con Chorizo y Papas • 51

BEEF WITH CHORIZO AND POTATOES

Carne con Nopales y Papas • 53

BEEF WITH ANCHO CHILES, CACTUS, AND POTATOES

Carne con Rajas • 54

SLOW COOKER FAJITAS

Although most people think of tacos and other street foods as typical Mexican fare, the heart and soul of Mexican regional cooking is actually the simple one-pot stew called a *guisado*.

There are hundreds, if not thousands, of variations, from the traditional to the modern, from the spicy beef and dried chiles of the north to the famous moles of central Mexico to pitch-black Yucatecan *mole negro* prepared with wild turkey. Whatever regional name they go by, *guisados* are really just thick, savory sauces cooked with tender pieces of slowly simmered meats.

As a general rule, the taste and texture of the sauce are at least as important as the meat. In the case of moles, the mole sauce *is* the dish; the meat is simply a garnish. Preparations flow from meal to meal, so the shredded chicken that flavored the morning's *caldo de pollo* is likely to reappear cloaked in dinner's *mole negro*. A substantial *guisado* might be served in a *cazuela* with rice, beans, and tortillas, or it can be used for stuffing chile rellenos or enchiladas, tucked into tacos or gorditas, or used to fill burritos and tamales.

These easy one-*cazuela* main dishes are perfect for the slow cooker. Some recipes will call for you to make a simple salsa before adding the meat for the final, slow cooking. By replicating the techniques that have been used by the cooks of Mexico for thousands of years—usually toasting, soaking, and pureeing—you can achieve an amazing depth of flavor and texture.

Pollo en Crema con Chipotles

CHICKEN AND PEPPERS IN CHIPOTLE CREAM ↓ Serves 6

Danny Esparza is the chef in charge of our daily "family meal" at SOL Cocina, and this smoky, creamy chicken recipe is one of his specialties. Instead of bone-in chicken breasts you can use boneless chicken pieces, if you like, in which case the cooking time will be shorter by as much as an hour. Don't be afraid of using both jalapeños and chipotles; the sauce, tempered by the cream, is only moderately spicy, and the jalapeños give a wonderful green chile savor to the sauce. Serve with corn tortillas and rice.

6 chicken breasts (about 4 pounds total)
1 cup water
2 teaspoons kosher salt
1 large white onion
1 tablespoon vegetable oil
2 large jalapeño chiles, stemmed, seeded, and cut into strips
1 large poblano chile, stemmed, seeded, and cut into strips
1 red bell pepper, stemmed, seeded, and cut into strips
1 large Roma tomato, diced
3 tablespoons minced garlic
$1/4$ cup finely chopped chipotles in adobo, or more to taste
$1/2$ teaspoon freshly ground black pepper
1 cup heavy cream

TO SERVE
Sliced Hass avocado

Place the chicken, water, and 1 teaspoon of the salt in a 5-quart slow cooker. Cover and cook on low, turning the chicken once, for 3 to 4 hours, or until the chicken is just tender.

When the chicken is cooked, remove from the slow cooker, leaving the broth in the cooker. Remove the bones and skin from the chicken and return the meat in large pieces to the slow cooker.

Peel the onion and cut in half horizontally. Cut a half-inch slice from the root and stem ends and discard. Stand the onion halves on their ends and cut $1/4$-inch slices from top to bottom.

Heat the oil in a large skillet over medium-high heat. Add the onion, chiles, bell pepper, tomato, garlic, and chipotles and cook, stirring frequently, until the vegetables begin to soften, about 5 minutes. Season with the remaining 1 teaspoon salt and the pepper. Reduce the heat slightly and continue to cook until the vegetables are just tender but still have a bit of bite. Add the cream and bring to a boil. Add the cream mixture to the chicken in the slow cooker. Cover and cook 1 hour on low.

Taste and adjust the seasoning before serving with the avocado slices.

VARIATIONS

• For a quick variation on this recipe, cook and debone the chicken as directed, then cook the onion, chiles, bell pepper, tomato, garlic, and chipotles as directed. Then, in a sauté pan, combine the chicken and vegetables. Add 2 cups of the cooking liquid from the slow cooker to the pan and simmer for 10 minutes, then add the cream and simmer 10 minutes more, until thickened.

• To tone down the heat, omit the chipotles and add 1 tablespoon soy bacon bits to the chicken in the slow cooker to add a little smoky savor. Substitute green bell pepper or Anaheim chiles for the poblanos and jalapeños.

Pollo en Salsa

CHICKEN IN TOMATO-JALAPEÑO SALSA ⤋ Serves 6

This dish is traditionally made with a whole chicken, which is cut into pieces and cooked slowly until tender. This results in a wonderful flavor, of course, but you can substitute boneless chicken if you prefer, which will also shorten the cooking time. The chicken finishes by simmering in a fresh tomato sauce, made medium-spicy with jalapeños. Turn up the heat by using *picante* serrano chiles, or substitute poblano or Anaheim chiles for great flavor but little or no heat. Serve with warm tortillas, beans and rice, or roasted potatoes to mop up all that wonderful sauce. Any leftover chicken, shredded in the sauce, makes an excellent filling for tacos, enchiladas, or tamales.

1 tablespoon fresh lard or vegetable oil
4 pounds chicken pieces (breasts, thighs, or a combination)
2 cups water
2 teaspoons kosher salt
8 large Roma tomatoes (about 2 pounds total)
4 large jalapeño chiles, stemmed and seeded
1/2 white onion, coarsely chopped
4 large cloves garlic

TO SERVE
Chopped fresh cilantro

In a large, heavy skillet, heat the lard over medium-high heat. Add the chicken pieces and cook, turning occasionally, until golden on all sides. In a 5- or 6-quart slow cooker, combine the chicken, water, and salt. Cover and cook on low for 4 hours, until the chicken is just tender.

Thirty minutes before the chicken is finished, combine the tomatoes, jalapeños, onion, and garlic in a 4-quart saucepan. Cover with water and bring to a boil over high heat. Reduce the heat to medium and simmer until the jalapeños are barely tender, about 5 minutes. Drain well, transfer to a blender, and puree until smooth.

Drain the chicken pieces, saving the broth for another use. Return the chicken to the slow cooker and pour the salsa over the chicken. Cover and cook for another 2 hours on low (or 1 hour on high), or until the chicken is tender but not falling apart and the salsa has thickened.

To serve, sprinkle the cilantro over the hot chicken.

VARIATIONS
- For a quick and easy variation on this recipe, puree the uncooked tomatoes and other vegetables with 1 cup water or chicken broth and 1 teaspoon salt. Pour over the chicken pieces in the slow cooker and cook on low for 6 hours.

- If you want to make this recipe ahead, cook and drain the chicken as directed and then refrigerate the chicken until needed. Thirty minutes before serving, make the salsa and pour it into a large skillet. Add the cooked chicken, cover, and simmer for 30 minutes, or until the chicken is heated through and the sauce has thickened slightly.

MOLES

The word *mole* refers a whole class of unique sauces for which Mexico is justly famed. Ancient moles, which incorporate local chiles, seeds, nuts, fruits, herbs, spices, bittersweet chocolate, and often corn—all of which are native to Mesoamerica—are the purest expression of Mexico's indigenous *terroir*. Using the most basic cooking implements—stones to crush and grind *(mole)*, fire, clay pots, and griddles—pre-Hispanic cooks toasted and pureed chiles, ground seeds, pounded fruits and vegetables, and simmered and strained, transforming these ingredients into smooth sauces of amazing richness and complexity. With the exception of imported spices such as clove, black pepper, and cumin, moles today are probably very similar to those of a thousand years ago.

In spite of their fearsome reputation for requiring long and complicated preparation, moles are really just thick sauces based on chiles, and there are many simple recipes and variations based on local ingredients and traditions. (The array of ingredients used for Mole Negro is pictured on page 34.)

It's important to understand that the mole sauce *is* the dish. So it's not chicken with mole sauce; it is a mole with chicken, and the meats are the garnish. The "big" moles, such as Mole Negro (page 41), are often served with tamales instead of meat.

The slow cooker makes moles with authentic flavor, without the multiple steps and hours of grinding, pureeing, frying, and simmering (not to mention pots to clean). An inexpensive food mill is essential for removing the skins and fibers from the sauce, which reduces bitterness and creates a velvety texture that drapes on the plate like a soft blanket.

As for the meat that will accompany the mole, a native wild turkey *(guajolote)* is most authentic. An heirloom breed of turkey would also do nicely, though both will take longer to cook than chicken. Free-range and kosher chickens are much tastier than your average supermarket chicken. For the best flavor, birds should always be cooked with the skin and bones. You can easily remove these, if you like, after the chicken is cooked.

Mole Negro

BLACK MOLE ⚖ Serves 6

Rich, thick, velvety smooth, and deeply colored, *mole negro* is the queen of moles. Making it can be a big production, too, a seemingly endless series of toasting, blackening, grinding, and frying to produce that mystically deep, almost black color. This slow cooker version is just as delicious and *much* easier. The tiny touch of chocolate at the end seems odd, but it is exactly the right amount of sweetness needed to balance the powerful chiles. You will taste the difference. Use any leftovers to make Enmoladas de Pollo (page 77). Or you may make the mole without the chicken (see Note) and pour the mole over tamales (page 88) or roast turkey.

6 chicken breasts or 12 chicken thighs
   (about 4 pounds)
5 chiles negros, stemmed and seeded
3 guajillo chiles, stemmed and seeded
2 large ancho chiles, stemmed and seeded
1 dried chipotle chile, stemmed and seeded
$1/2$ white onion, diced
5 large garlic cloves, peeled
$1^1/2$ Roma tomatoes, diced
2 large tomatillos, husked, washed, and diced
$1/2$ firm banana, peeled and cubed
2 tablespoons whole almonds
2 tablespoons raw peanuts
$1/4$ cup sesame seeds
$1/4$ cup seedless raisins
$1/4$ teaspoon ground cinnamon
$1/4$ teaspoon whole black peppercorns
3 whole cloves
1 teaspoon whole anise seed
2 teaspoons whole dried Mexican oregano
$1/4$ teaspoon dried thyme
2 teaspoons kosher salt
4 cups Caldo de Pollo (page 95), or more as
   needed
1 tablespoon crushed Ibarra Mexican chocolate

TO SERVE
Toasted sesame seeds

Place all the ingredients except the chicken and chocolate in a 5-quart slow cooker. Set the chicken on top. Cover and cook on low for 4 hours, or until the chicken is tender but not falling off the bone. Remove the chicken. If you like, you can remove the skin and bones now, or you can serve it as is, which is the traditional way. Set the chicken on a warm platter covered with aluminum foil to keep warm while you finish the mole.

Transfer contents of slow cooker to a blender. Add the chocolate and blend on high for several minutes, until perfectly smooth. Check the seasoning; moles should taste slightly underseasoned, and never salty. The mole should be thick and very smooth. For a velvety texture, pass the sauce through a food mill to remove any remaining skins and fibers. If necessary, add a little water or broth to thin the sauce to a coating consistency.

To serve, liberally ladle the mole over the chicken, then lightly dust with the sesame seeds.

NOTE
The sauce can be cooked without the chicken, but if you do, make it with Caldo de Pollo (page 95) for the best flavor. The mole can also be made meatless, using vegetable stock, for a vegetarian version.

Mole Manchamanteles

RED MOLE WITH CHICKEN AND FRIED PLANTAINS ↙ Serves 6

In this simple mole, deep flavored ancho chiles balance the sweetness of the fresh fruit that forms the base of the sauce. The name means "tablecloth stainer," a tribute to both the gluttonous abandon induced by this luscious sauce and its deep red color. The recipe calls for chicken, but you can cook the sauce without the meat (using chicken broth for the best flavor) and serve it with roasted vegetables, turkey, Cornish hens, duck, tamales, or pork carnitas instead. Manchamanteles is usually served with plain white rice, dusted with sesame seeds and sprinkled with bit of ripe pineapple. The fried plantains (*tostones*) are a delicious addition.

6 chicken breasts or 12 chicken thighs
   (about 4 pounds)
4 ancho chiles, stemmed and seeded
1 cup peeled, diced fresh pineapple (see Note)
1/2 apple, peeled and diced
1/4 cup whole shelled almonds
1/4 cup seedless raisins
3 cloves garlic, peeled
1/2 white onion, diced
2 small Roma tomatoes, diced
1/4 teaspoon whole black peppercorns
2 whole cloves
1 tablespoon sesame seeds
1 dried bay leaf
1/4 teaspoon ground cinnamon
2 teaspoons whole dried Mexican oregano
2 teaspoons kosher salt
2 1/2 cups Caldo de Pollo (page 95) or water,
   or more as needed

TO SERVE
Toasted sesame seeds
3/4 cup peeled, finely diced fresh pineapple
   (see Note)
Fried Plantains (recipe follows)

Place all the ingredients except the chicken in a 5-quart slow cooker, and set the chicken on top. Cover and cook on low for 3 to 4 hours, or until the chicken is tender but not falling off the bone.

Remove the chicken. If you like, you can remove the skin and bones now, or you can serve it as is. Set the chicken on a warm platter covered with aluminum foil to keep warm while you finish the mole.

Transfer the remaining contents of the slow cooker to a blender. Blend on high for several minutes, until perfectly smooth. If the sauce seems too thick, add a little more chicken broth or water and blend again. Taste and add a pinch of salt if necessary, remembering that moles are rich and thick but are never highly seasoned. For the perfect texture, pass the sauce through a food mill, but it is perfectly acceptable straight out of the blender.

To serve, liberally ladle the mole over the chicken. Lightly dust with the sesame seeds and garnish each serving with a few pieces of pineapple and fried plantain.

NOTE
Canned pineapple may be substituted for fresh as long as it is well drained. If you are using it as a garnish, sauté the pieces quickly in a hot pan until dry and almost caramelized.

continued

Fried Plantains

For the best results, use soft, ripe plantains with black skin.

2 large, ripe plantains
About $1/3$ cup vegetable oil
Kosher or sea salt

Peel the plantains and cut into rounds 1 inch thick. Heat $1/4$ inch of oil in a small, heavy skillet. Working in batches, fry the plantains on both sides until a light brown crust forms. Remove and let cool slightly, then flatten gently with a spatula to a thickness of $1/2$ inch. Return the plantains to the oil and cook until brown. Drain well on paper towels and serve warm, sprinkled with a few grains of salt.

Costillos

PORK RIBS IN CHIPOTLE-TOMATILLO SALSA ↓ Serves 6

This easy recipe consists of succulent braised ribs in a light sauce that has just the right kick of smokiness and heat. *Costillos* are pork rib tips, only a couple of inches long, with plenty of juicy meat. They are similar to country-style ribs, which may be substituted. The same salsa is terrific cooked with boneless pork shoulder, pork chops, or chicken. You can add peeled cubed potatoes or zucchini to the slow cooker with the meat, or roast red potatoes with oil and salt to serve alongside this dish. If you have a second slow cooker, Pan de Elote (page 110) would be delicious with the spicy ribs.

$4^1/2$ pounds small costillos (see above)
    or country-style pork ribs
2 large Roma tomatoes, diced
1 (7-ounce) can chipotles in adobo
$1/2$ white onion, diced
$1/3$ cup garlic cloves
4 tomatillos
2 teaspoons kosher salt

TO SERVE
Warm corn tortillas

Cut the ribs into pieces 3 inches long and place in a 5-quart slow cooker.

In a blender, combine the remaining ingredients and puree until smooth. Pour over the ribs, cover, and cook on low for 6 hours.

Serve hot with the warm tortillas.

Asado de Bodas

WEDDING STEW WITH PORK ⩗ *Serves 6*

Asado de bodas is definitely something special, as befits a wedding feast. Recipes with this name vary from north to south and east to west. Some use only ancho chiles, while others are made with beef instead of pork, but all incorporate that touch of sweet and sour, cloves, and cinnamon, along with just a hint of orange and chocolate, an influence from medieval convents. Toasting the whole spices and grinding them just before cooking is a simple step that adds wonderful flavor. Another small step that makes a difference is mincing the onions almost to a pulp, so that they melt into the sauce. Serve with simple white rice and warm flour tortillas.

4 large guajillo chiles, stemmed and seeded
2 ancho or pasilla chiles, stemmed and seeded
2 cups hot water
4 large cloves garlic, peeled
2 teaspoons kosher salt
1/2 teaspoon whole cumin seeds
1 whole clove
1/2 teaspoon whole black peppercorns
2 pounds boneless pork shoulder, cut into
   1-inch cubes
1 cup very finely minced white onion
1/2 teaspoon dried marjoram
1 dried bay leaf
1-inch piece cinnamon stick or 1/4 teaspoon
   ground cinnamon
1 cup water, Caldo de Pollo (page 95), or
   Caldo de Res (page 96)
1 teaspoon white vinegar
1 teaspoon firmly packed piloncillo or brown
   sugar
1 teaspoon grated orange zest
1 tablespoon grated Ibarra Mexican chocolate
   or semisweet chocolate

Heat a heavy skillet over medium-high heat. Add the chiles and toast on both sides, turning occasionally and pressing down with a spatula, until they soften and blister. Remove from the pan. Place in a heatproof bowl and pour the hot water over them. Soak for 15 minutes, stirring once. Drain, reserving 1 cup of the soaking liquid.

In a blender, combine the chiles and the reserved soaking liquid, garlic, and salt and puree until perfectly smooth.

In a small skillet over medium heat, toast the cumin, clove, and peppercorns until fragrant, stirring frequently so they don't burn. Let cool completely and grind in a spice grinder.

Place the pork in the bottom of a 5-quart slow cooker and sprinkle with the ground spices. Add the onion, marjoram, bay leaf, and cinnamon. Pour the chile puree over the meat and add the water. Stir well. Cover and cook on low 6 hours, stirring once or twice, until the meat is tender and the sauce is thick and fragrant.

Remove and discard the bay leaf and cinnamon stick. Stir in the vinegar, piloncillo, orange zest, and chocolate. Serve hot.

Chile Verde

PORK IN GREEN CHILE SALSA ⤋ *Serves 6*

Salsa chile verde takes its name from three types of green chiles, which are combined with green tomatillos to make an olive-green sauce with a gently tart and spicy edge. Never overpowering, it's a perfect match for the richness of the pork. You can control the level of heat by adding more jalapeños, substituting spicier serrano chiles, or leaving out the hot chiles altogether. For frying the pork, I like to use flavorful fresh (liquid) lard, called *asiento*, which I buy at my local Latin grocery. (I also save the fat from Carnitas, on page 98, for the same purpose.) All the ingredients go into the slow cooker hot, so the dish cooks in about 2 hours. This recipe is excellent with made with *chuletas* (pork chops) instead of diced pork. Serve with rice, beans, and warm corn tortillas.

2 teaspoons whole cumin seeds
1 whole clove
1 teaspoon whole black peppercorns
10 tomatillos (about 12 ounces total), husked and washed
2 jalapeño chiles, stemmed
8 Anaheim chiles, roasted (see page 5), seeded, and diced
4 large cloves garlic
2½ teaspoons kosher salt
2 tablespoons fresh lard or vegetable oil
2½ pounds boneless pork shoulder, cut into ¾-inch cubes
2 large poblano chiles, roasted (see page 5), seeded, and diced
½ white onion, finely diced
1 cup water, Caldo de Pollo (page 95), or Caldo de Res (page 96)
1 dried bay leaf

TO SERVE
Mexican crema

In a small skillet over medium heat, toast the cumin, clove, and peppercorns until fragrant, stirring frequently so they don't burn. Let cool completely and grind in a spice grinder.

Place the tomatillos and jalapeños in a small saucepan and cover with cold water. Bring to a boil and simmer 5 minutes, or until barely soft. Drain immediately and place in a food processor along with the Anaheim chiles, garlic, and salt. Pulse until smooth.

Heat the lard in a large skillet over medium-high heat and, working in batches, brown the pork on one side without stirring the meat, then turn and brown on the other side. Return all the pork to the skillet and add the poblanos and onion and cook, stirring, until the onions are soft, about 5 minutes. Add the ground spices and cook, stirring, for an additional 2 minutes, until the spices are fragrant. Transfer the pork mixture to a 5-quart slow cooker.

Reduce the skillet heat to medium. Add the contents of the food processor to the pan and cook, stirring, until the salsa is thick and begins to stick to the pan. Add the water and bay leaf to the pan and simmer, stirring once or twice, for 5 minutes. Stir into the pork in the slow cooker, cover, and cook on low 2 hours, or until the pork is tender.

Serve hot with a bowl of *crema* alongside.

NOTE
Leftovers make an excellent filling for tamales.

Carne Pibil

PORK IN BANANA LEAVES WITH ACHIOTE ⩊ Serves 6

The vibrant red color and distinctive flavor of this recipe come from the *achiote recado,* a spice paste made with annatto, the seed of a tree native to Central America. Long, slow cooking in banana leaves brings a taste of tropical Mexico to your slow cooker while replicating the traditional pit-cooking method that gives the recipe its name. Keep it simple and authentic by serving it with black beans, corn tortillas, and white rice, as well as fiery Mayan *xni pec,* a citrusy salsa laced with onion and habanero chiles. Fried plantains (page 44) are an excellent accompaniment as well. Boneless chicken may be used instead of the pork shoulder.

2 teaspoons whole cumin seeds
3 ounces achiote paste
1/4 cup peeled garlic cloves
2 serrano chiles, stemmed
1/2 cup diced white onion
2 teaspoons kosher salt
2 tablespoons white vinegar
2 tablespoons fresh orange juice
2 1/2 pounds boneless pork shoulder,
    cut into 1-inch cubes
2 (12-inch) pieces banana or plantain leaf
    (see Note)
1/2 cup water

TO SERVE
Chopped fresh cilantro
Xni Pec Salsa (recipe follows)

In a small skillet over medium heat, toast the cumin until fragrant, stirring frequently so it doesn't burn. Let cool completely and grind in a spice grinder.

Combine the ground cumin with the achiote paste, garlic, serranos, onion, salt, vinegar, and orange juice in a food processor and process until very smooth. Coat the pork evenly with half of the spice mixture.

Line the bottom of a slow cooker with one piece of banana leaf. Top with the pork and the remaining spice mixture. Add the water and place the second banana leaf over the pork. Cover and cook on low for 8 hours.

Serve with chopped cilantro and the salsa.

NOTE
Fresh banana and plantain leaves can be found at Latin groceries. They should be washed and dried before use. Frozen banana leaves can usually be found in Asian markets.

Xni Pec Salsa

MAKES 3/4 CUP

Habanero chiles are extremely *picante.* It takes time for the full impact of the heat to travel through the salsa, so it's wise to start with a small amount then taste again before adding more.

1/2 small red onion, diced
1 small Roma tomato, diced
1/2 teaspoon seeded and minced habanero chile
1 tablespoon fresh lime juice
1 tablespoon fresh orange juice
1 teaspoon white vinegar
1/4 teaspoon kosher salt
1 tablespoon finely chopped fresh cilantro

Combine all ingredients in a small bowl. Let stand for 15 minutes, then adjust seasoning with salt and more habanero, if necessary.

Albondigas en Salsa Chipotle

MEATBALLS IN CHIPOTLE SAUCE ⭨ Serves 6

Albondigas (meatballs) are easy to make and festive enough for a buffet or party. The chipotle salsa is as simple as can be, and the whole thing simmers away until you are ready to serve it. Serve the *albondigas* in big bowls, garnished with creamy diced avocado and a sprinkling of crunchy *chicharrón*. Rice is the classic accompaniment.

3/4 pound ground pork
3/4 pound ground beef
2 large eggs, beaten
1/4 cup fresh bread crumbs
2 cloves garlic
1 teaspoon kosher salt
1 teaspoon freshly ground black pepper
1 teaspoon ground cumin
1 sprig fresh flat-leaf parsley, or 2 sprigs
   fresh cilantro, finely chopped
Caldo de Res (page 96), as needed

CHIPOTLE SALSA
8 whole Roma tomatoes (about 2 pounds total)
2 large cloves garlic, peeled
1 teaspoon ground cumin
1 (7-ounce) can chipotles in adobo
1 tablespoon whole dried Mexican oregano
1 cup water or Caldo de Res (page 96)
2 tablespoons fresh lard or vegetable oil

TO SERVE
Diced Hass avocado
Crumbled chicharrón

In a large bowl, thoroughly mix the pork, beef, and eggs with your hands. In a food processor, combine the bread crumbs, garlic, salt, pepper, cumin, and parsley and pulse until combined.

Add to the meat mixture and stir to combine. Divide the meat mixture into 12 or 24 equal portions, roll into balls, and chill for 30 minutes while you make the salsa.

To make the salsa, line a heavy skillet with aluminum foil and set over high heat. Add the tomatoes to the skillet and char on all sides, turning as little as possible, until blackened and soft. Place the tomatoes in a blender with the garlic, cumin, chipotles, oregano, and water. Puree until completely smooth, about 1 minute. For a smoother texture, you can pass the sauce through a fine-mesh sieve or food mill, if you like.

In a saucepan, heat the lard over medium heat. Add the salsa and cook, stirring, until slightly thickened, about 5 minutes.

Place the meatballs in the bottom of the slow cooker. Pour the salsa over, cover, and cook for 3 1/2 hours on low.

Divide the meatballs among 6 large bowls. Thin the sauce, if necessary, with a little broth and spoon over the meatballs. Garnish with the diced avocado and crumble a few pieces of *chicharrón* over each bowl.

Carne con Chorizo y Papas

BEEF WITH CHORIZO AND POTATOES ↓ *Serves 6*

A different take on meat and potatoes, this easy, spicy *guisado* is made with chorizo, tender beef, potatoes, plenty of garlic, and spicy chiles de árbol. Be sure to buy *Mexican* chorizo, which is a soft uncured sausage flavored with chiles, garlic, cumin, and marjoram. Beef chorizo tastes the same as the pork version, and both are available at Latin markets. Serve the *guisado* with rice and flour tortillas, or use it as a filling for burritos or *sopes* (see page 61). To reduce the heat, cut back on the chiles de árbol.

12 guajillo chiles, stemmed and seeded
2 ancho chiles, stemmed and seeded
10 chiles de árbol, stemmed and seeded
6 cups hot water
4 cloves garlic
2 teaspoons kosher salt
2 cups peeled and diced red potatoes
2 pounds boneless beef chuck, cut into
   1-inch cubes
8 ounces beef or pork chorizo, crumbled
1/2 white onion, very finely minced
2 teaspoons whole dried Mexican oregano
1 cup water, Caldo de Pollo (page 95), or
   Caldo de Res (page 96)

TO SERVE
Diced white onion
Mexican crema or sour cream (optional)

Heat a heavy skillet over medium-high heat. Add the chiles and toast on both sides, turning occasionally and pressing down with a spatula, until they soften and blister. Remove from the pan. When the chiles are cool enough to handle, tear them into small pieces and place in a heatproof bowl. Add the hot water and soak the chiles, stirring occasionally, for 15 minutes. Drain, reserving 1 1/2 cups of the soaking liquid.

In a blender, combine the chiles with the reserved soaking liquid, garlic, and salt and puree until perfectly smooth, scraping down the sides several times.

Place the potatoes in the bottom of a 5-quart slow cooker. Layer the beef over the potatoes. Crumble the chorizo over the beef. Add the onion and oregano. Pour the chile puree and water over the meat.

Cover and cook on low for 6 hours, stirring several times, until the meat is tender. The sauce might begin to separate, but this will not affect the taste.

Serve hot, sprinkled with the diced onion, and dollop with *crema*, if you like.

Carne con Nopales y Papas

BEEF WITH ANCHO CHILES, CACTUS, AND POTATOES ↙ Serves 6

This thick, delicious *guisado* comes from the rugged state of San Luis Potosí, where the ancient and distinctive regional cuisine is based on the local desert plants. Nopales, the paddles from beavertail cactus (also called prickly pear cactus), are readily available at Mexican markets. Buy fresh nopales, which must be boiled before eating, rather than the canned variety. Once cooked, they have a taste and texture much like cooked green beans. You can substitute pork for the beef, or Mexican calabaza squash for the potatoes, if you like.

6 ancho chiles, stemmed and seeded
3 cups hot water
2 Roma tomatoes
2 cloves garlic, peeled
1 tablespoon fresh lard
2 pounds boneless beef chuck, cut into
   1-inch pieces
1 1/2 teaspoons kosher salt
1 teaspoon freshly ground black pepper
2 cups Caldo de Res (page 96) or Caldo de Pollo
   (page 95)
1 white onion, diced
6 tomatillos, husked, washed, and diced
2 small red potatoes, peeled and diced
1/2 teaspoon whole dried Mexican oregano
8 ounces cleaned nopales, cut into 1/2-inch pieces

TO SERVE
   Warm corn tortillas
   Diced white onion
   Chopped fresh cilantro

Heat a heavy skillet over medium-high heat. Add the chiles and toast on both sides, turning occasionally and pressing down with a spatula, until they soften and blister. Remove from the pan. When the chiles are cool enough to handle, tear them into small pieces and place in a heatproof bowl. Add the hot water and soak the chiles, stirring occasionally, for 15 minutes. Drain, reserving 1 cup of the soaking liquid.

Line the skillet with a piece of aluminum foil and roast the tomatoes on all sides over medium-high heat, until softened and charred in places. In a blender, combine the tomatoes, ancho chiles and garlic and puree until perfectly smooth, adding a little of the reserved soaking liquid as needed.

Heat the lard in a heavy skillet and brown the beef on all sides until dark brown, working in batches so you don't crowd the pan. Place the beef in a 5-quart slow cooker and add the salt and pepper. Add the chile puree to the skillet and cook over medium heat, stirring and scraping, until the puree is thickened and bubbling, about 5 minutes. Add the broth, stir well to combine, and simmer for 5 minutes. Pour the chile mixture over the beef in the slow cooker and add the onion, tomatillos, potatoes, and oregano. Cover and cook on low for 5 hours.

At least 30 minutes before serving, place the nopales in a small saucepan, cover with cold water, and bring to a boil over high heat. Boil for 15 minutes, then drain and rinse well with cold water. Fifteen minutes before serving, stir the nopales into the slow cooker to heat through.

Serve hot with the tortillas, with the diced onion and cilantro on the side.

Carne con Rajas

SLOW COOKER FAJITAS ↘ *Serves 6*

They simmer instead of sizzle, but these slow cooker "fajitas" will quickly become a favorite. The jalapeños are seeded, so they are only mildly spicy, but poblano or Anaheim chiles would be a good substitute. Serve with sliced avocado, cotija cheese, northern-style flour tortillas and, of course, beans and rice.

2$^1\!/_2$ pounds boneless beef chuck, in
    one thick piece
2 tablespoons fresh lard or vegetable oil
2$^1\!/_2$ teaspoons kosher salt
1 teaspoon freshly ground black pepper
5 sprigs fresh cilantro
4 cloves garlic, sliced, plus 1 tablespoon
    minced garlic
$^1\!/_2$ cup Caldo de Res (page 96)
$^1\!/_2$ white onion, sliced $^1\!/_2$ inch thick
6 to 8 large jalapeño chiles
1 red onion
1 red bell pepper
Leaves from 2 sprigs fresh epazote

TO SERVE
Sliced Hass avocado
Warm flour tortillas
Crumbled cotija cheese

Slice the beef into long strips about 1 inch thick. Heat 1 tablespoon of the lard in a heavy skillet over medium-high heat and brown the beef on all sides until dark brown. Place the beef in a 5-quart slow cooker along with 2 teaspoons of the salt, the pepper, cilantro, the sliced garlic, and the broth.

In the same skillet, fry the white onion over medium-high heat, stirring very little, until it is dark brown, or even slightly charred. Add the onion to the slow cooker. Scrape up any small bits from the pan and add those to the slow cooker as well. Cover and cook on low for 4 hours, or until the meat is tender.

Line a heavy skillet with a piece of aluminum foil. Add the jalapeños to the skillet and roast on all sides over medium-high heat until slightly charred and softened. Remove the stems, cut each jalapeño into 4 pieces lengthwise, and remove the seeds.

Peel the red onion and cut $^1\!/_2$ inch off the stem and root ends. Cut in half vertically, from the stem end to the root end. Set one onion half on the root end and slice from top to bottom to create $^1\!/_2$-inch wide crescents of onion. Repeat with the remaining onion half.

Core and trim the red bell pepper and cut into pieces $^1\!/_2$ inch wide and 3 inches long.

When the meat is cooked, and about 30 minutes before you want to serve, heat the remaining 1 tablespoon lard or oil in a heavy skillet over medium-high heat. Add the red onion, jalapeños, red pepper, and epazote, and cook, stirring often, until the onions are almost soft, about 5 minutes. Season with the remaining $^1\!/_2$ teaspoon salt. Add the minced garlic and cook for 1 minute. Add the onion mixture to the slow cooker, stir in carefully, and cook, covered, for 15 minutes.

Top with the avocado and serve with warm flour tortillas and a small bowl of cotija cheese on the side.

Street Food Favorites

Basic Masa for Tortillas,
Quesadillas, Sopes, and More • 62

Masa Verde • 63
JALAPEÑO-CILANTRO MASA

'Tinga Tostada • 64
CHICKEN WITH CHIPOTLES AND ONION
ON CRISP TOSTADAS

Tacos de Pollo • 66
SOFT TACOS WITH CHICKEN AND SALSA MEXICANA

Tacos de Pollo Deshebrado • 67
QUICK SHREDDED CHICKEN TACOS

Tacos de Res Dorado • 69
CRISP SHREDDED BEEF TACOS WITH
ROASTED TOMATO SALSA

Picadillo • 70
SOFT TACOS WITH BEEF, GREEN CHILE,
CUMIN, AND POTATO

Tacos de Mixiote • 72
TACOS OF LAMB BRAISED WITH CHILES

Tacos de Carnitas • 73
SLOW-COOKED PORK TACOS WITH SALSA VERDE

Enchiladas Suizas • 74
CHICKEN AND CHEESE ENCHILADAS
WITH SALSA VERDE

Enchiladas en Salsa Roja • 76
BEEF ENCHILADAS IN RED CHILE SAUCE

Enmoladas de Pollo • 77
CHICKEN WITH MOLE NEGRO

Burrito Ahogado • 79
"WET" CHICKEN AND RICE BURRITO WITH
FRESH TOMATO AND GUAJILLO SALSA

Burrito "El Güero" • 81
BEEF AND BEAN BURRITO WITH CHEESE

Burrito de Carnitas • 82
BRAISED PORK BURRITO WITH SALSA VERDE
AND AVOCADO-TOMATO SALSA

Burrito con Carne Colorado
"El Norte" • 83
BEEF BURRITO IN SPICY RED CHILE SAUCE

Tamales • 88

Torta de Tamal • 90
TAMAL PIE

'Tinga Tostada

CHICKEN WITH CHIPOTLES AND ONION ON CRISP TOSTADAS ⅃ Serves 6 (makes 12 tostadas)

'Tinga has no meaning—except maybe "delicious." Here shredded chicken is combined with a smoky chipotle salsa and strips of sautéed onion. It's a perfect potluck or party dish, as guests can build their own tostadas, heaping on the chicken and adding some diced avocado and a little Mexican *crema*. 'Tinga is also excellent on *sopes* (see page 61) or wrapped up in enchiladas and burritos. The "pole-to-pole" technique of slicing onions described here produces curved strips of onion that keep their shape and texture when cooked. The chicken and salsa can be made well ahead of time, refrigerated, and then reheated when you are ready to serve.

2¹/₂ pounds boneless, skinless chicken thighs
1 cup water
2 teaspoons kosher salt
4 Roma tomatoes
1 pound tomatillos, husked and washed
   (about 16 small)
1 jalapeño chile, stemmed and halved lengthwise
3 large cloves garlic, peeled
2 to 4 canned chipotles in adobo
2 large white onions
1 tablespoon vegetable oil
1 teaspoon whole dried Mexican oregano

TO SERVE
Round corn tostadas (see Note)
Diced Hass avocado
Mexican crema

Place the chicken in the slow cooker and add the water and 1 teaspoon of the salt. Cover and cook on low for 4 hours, or until just tender.

While the chicken cooks, make the salsa. In a 2-quart saucepan combine the tomatoes, tomatillos, and jalapeño. Cover with cold water, bring to a boil over high heat, then reduce the heat to a simmer. Simmer until the tomatillos are barely tender, about 5 minutes. Drain the vegetables well and transfer them to a blender along with the garlic, chipotles, and the remaining 1 teaspoon salt. Blend until fairly smooth and refrigerate the salsa until needed.

Peel the onions and cut ¹/₂ inch off the stem and root ends. Cut each onion in half vertically. Set one onion half on the root end and cut from top to bottom to create ¹/₄-inch slices. Repeat with the remaining onion halves.

When the chicken is cooked, remove it from the slow cooker and break it into large pieces. Strain the cooking liquid, discarding the solids, and reserve for another use.

Heat the oil in a large, heavy frying pan over medium heat. Add the onions and oregano and cook, stirring often, until the onions are soft but not browned, about 5 minutes. Add the salsa and chicken to the pan and simmer for 5 minutes, or until heated through.

To serve, pile the chicken mixture on tostadas and top with the avocado and *crema*.

NOTE
Available in all Mexican markets, tostadas are 4- or 5-inch round corn tortillas that are fried until crisp. They are often sold in stacks labeled as *tostadas caseras*.

Tacos de Res Dorado

CRISP SHREDDED BEEF TACOS WITH ROASTED TOMATO SALSA ⭲ Makes 12 tacos

Simple, but so good! A *dorado* taco is crisped a bit on a lightly oiled griddle before being filled, in this case with succulent shredded beef. This is another perfect dish for a crowd, as most of the preparation can be done ahead of time. Serve the filled tacos on a platter with the garnishes on the side.

1 tablespoon vegetable oil, plus more for
   toasting the tortillas
1/2 cup white onion
4 cloves garlic, minced
1 serrano chile, stemmed and finely minced
   (or more to taste)
2 Roma tomatoes, finely diced
Shredded Beef (page 97)
Kosher salt
1/2 cup Caldo de Res (page 96) or reserved cooking liquid from the Shredded Beef (page 97)
12 corn tortillas

TO SERVE
Roasted Tomato Salsa (recipe follows) or
   salsa of your choice
Crumbled cotija cheese
Shredded lettuce
Diced white onions
Mexican crema or sour cream
Pickled jalapeños (optional)

Heat 1 tablespoon of the oil in a large skillet over medium-high heat. Add the onion, garlic, serrano, and tomatoes. Cook, stirring, until the onions are soft and the pan is dry, about 5 minutes. Add the beef and cook, stirring, for 2 minutes. Add the broth and simmer until the beef is moist and most of the broth has been absorbed. Taste and add salt, if needed. Keep warm.

Heat a *comal* or nonstick griddle over medium-high heat. Brush one side of a tortilla with oil and place it, oiled side down, on the hot surface. Toast until somewhat crisp but still flexible.

Place 2 to 3 tablespoons of shredded beef in the middle of the tortilla and fold in half. Serve hot with the salsa, cheese, lettuce, onions, *crema*, and jalapeños on the side.

Roasted Tomato Salsa

MAKES 1 1/2 CUPS

This is a terrific all-purpose salsa that I always have on hand. Sometimes I add a few drops of fresh lime juice to this salsa to perk up the flavors.

Double the recipe for a crowd.

3 ripe Roma tomatoes
1 unpeeled clove garlic
1 serrano chile
1/4 small white onion, coarsely chopped
4 to 6 sprigs fresh cilantro
1/2 teaspoon kosher salt

Line a heavy skillet with a piece of aluminum foil and heat over medium-high heat. Add the tomatoes, garlic, and serrano and roast until the skins are blackened and the vegetables are soft. Peel the garlic, stem the serrano, and transfer all the roasted vegetables to a food processor. Add the onion, cilantro, and salt and pulse until the salsa is fairly smooth but still has some texture. If it seems too thick, add a very small amount of water, then taste and adjust the seasoning if necessary.

Tacos de Mixiote

TACOS OF LAMB BRAISED WITH CHILES ↙ Serves 6

Mixiotes are little packets of braised meat and spices. They used to be cooked wrapped in agave leaves, but these days aluminum foil stands in for the endangered wild plant, as boneless lamb shoulder takes the place of goat. *Mixiotes* are meant to be savory, with a powerful flavor of chiles, which makes it the perfect filling for tacos or *sopes* (see page 61), where a little meat goes a long way. These tacos are wonderful paired with good mezcal or tequila.

5 guajillo chiles, stemmed and seeded (see Note)
5 ancho chiles, stemmed and seeded (see Note)
2 allspice berries
1 whole clove
$1/2$ teaspoon whole cumin seeds
$1/2$ teaspoon whole black peppercorns
2 dried bay leaves
1 teaspoon dried marjoram
$1/4$ teaspoon ground cinnamon
$1/4$ white onion, minced to a pulp
6 cloves garlic, very finely minced
1 tablespoon vegetable oil
$1/3$ cup white vinegar
$1/4$ cup water
2 tablespoons red achiote paste
4 pounds boneless lamb stew meat or shoulder, cut into $1^1/_2$-inch pieces
$1/4$ cup vegetable shortening

TO SERVE
Warm corn tortillas
Diced white onion
Chopped fresh cilantro
Arroz Mexicana (page 101)

Preheat the oven to 350°F. Spread the chiles on a baking sheet and toast in the oven until dry and crisp, 15 to 20 minutes. Let cool completely, then grind the chiles in a spice grinder. Transfer to a medium mixing bowl.

Heat a small sauté pan over medium heat. Add the allspice, clove, cumin, peppercorns, and bay leaf and toast until fragrant. Let cool completely, then grind in a spice grinder. Add to the bowl with the ground chiles along with the marjoram and cinnamon. Add the onion, garlic, oil, vinegar, and water. Crumble the achiote paste into the bowl. Stir to create a thick paste. Add the lamb and, using your hands, rub the marinade into the meat.

Rub the shortening on the bottom and 2 inches up the sides of a 5-quart slow cooker. Cut two pieces of aluminum foil, each about 24 inches long. Tuck one piece into the slow cooker with the ends hanging over the side. Press it flush against the sides and into the edges of the slow cooker. Place the other piece of foil at a right angle to the first and press it into the corners.

Transfer the lamb and marinade to the cooker. Fold together the ends of the inner piece of foil and roll down to within 1 inch of the lamb, leaving a small amount of space. Fold and roll the outer piece of foil at a right angle to the first to loosely seal the packet. Cover and cook on low for 6 hours.

To serve, spoon the hot lamb mixture onto the tortillas and top with the onion and cilantro. Serve the rice on the side.

NOTE
It you like, you can substitute ground ancho and guajillo chiles, which are sold at Mexican markets. Substitute 4 tablespoons of each kind of ground chile for the whole chiles. Be sure the product is pure ground chile, and not chile powder, which may contain other spices.

Tacos de Carnitas

SLOW-COOKED PORK TACOS WITH SALSA VERDE ↙ Serves 6

Carnitas is a specialty item in Mexico, made by simmering a whole pig in a vast copper cauldron until the various cuts are tender and succulent. On a smaller scale, however, carnitas can easily be made in a slow cooker with excellent results. Carnitas is delicious right from the slow cooker, but if it is chilled overnight, much of the fat can be removed before reheating it (save this fresh lard, or *asiento,* for sautéing). The meat will also be even moister and tastier the next day. It is delicious served on a gordita (see page 61) or *huarache* (see page 61).

Carnitas (page 98)

TO SERVE
Warm corn tortillas
Salsa Verde (page 74)
Diced red or white onion mixed with
    chopped fresh cilantro
Diced Hass avocado
Crumbled chicharrón (optional)

Remove the excess fat from the cooked carnitas and break into large chunks. Reheat the carnitas in its juices in a large skillet or in 350°F oven, until almost all the juices are absorbed. You may prefer it juicy and soft (in which case cover the meat as it reheats) or drier and crisp around the edges (reheat uncovered). To serve, spoon the hot carnitas on the tortillas and top with the salsa, onion, avocado, and *chicharrón.*

Enchiladas Suizas

CHICKEN AND CHEESE ENCHILADAS WITH SALSA VERDE ⤓ Makes 16 enchiladas

Tender chicken and melted cheese under a green tomatillo salsa create a very rich and subtle dish, a Mexican classic. Creamy and almost too soft to grate, Chihuahua cheese (also known as *menonita*) melts beautifully at low temperatures. Monterey jack, mild Gouda, or Muenster will also work if you can't find the Mexican import. For the most exquisite results, assemble the enchiladas with warm ingredients, bake briefly, and serve immediately.

Shredded Chicken (page 97)
1¹/₂ cups shredded Chihuaua (menonita) cheese
Vegetable oil for frying
16 day-old yellow corn tortillas
Salsa Verde (recipe follows), kept warm

TO SERVE
Crumbled cotija cheese
Mexican crema

Preheat the oven to 350°F. In a bowl, stir together the chicken and 1 cup of the cheese.

Pour ¹/₈ inch of oil in a small frying pan and heat over medium-high heat. Fry the tortillas, turning once, until they start to brown around the edges but are still flexible, adding oil to the pan as needed between batches. Fill each tortilla with about ¹/₄ cup of the chicken and cheese mixture and roll up. Arrange the enchiladas in a single layer in a baking dish.

Scatter the remaining ¹/₂ cup cheese over the enchiladas and bake until hot, about 10 minutes. Top with the warmed salsa.

To serve, dust with a little cotija cheese and drizzle with the *crema*.

Salsa Verde

MAKES 2 CUPS

12 ounces tomatillos, husked and washed (about 10)
¹/₂ small white onion, diced
1 large jalapeño chile, stemmed and chopped
1 clove garlic
1 teaspoon kosher salt
12 sprigs fresh cilantro, coarsely chopped

Combine the tomatillos, onion, jalapeño, and garlic in a small saucepan. Add water to cover and bring to a boil over high heat. Reduce the heat to a simmer and simmer until the tomatillos are soft but not falling apart, about 15 minutes.

Drain the vegetables and transfer to a blender. Puree until smooth, add the salt and cilantro, and pulse several times. If the sauce seems too thick, thin with a little water.

Enchiladas en Salsa Roja

BEEF ENCHILADAS IN RED CHILE SAUCE ↓ **Makes 16 enchiladas**

Enchiladas are one of the simplest Mexican dishes: the name simply means "in chile." (Similarly, *entomatadas* are dipped in tomato sauce, *enfrijoladas* in pureed beans, and *enmoladas* in mole sauce.) Like so many simple dishes, they are best freshly made and quickly consumed. These enchiladas are hearty and satisfying, so don't overload them. Have everything ready and hot before you start assembling the enchiladas. Serve them as they do in Mexico, fresh from the sauce, with a sprinkle of grated cheese, some shredded lettuce and onions, and a dab of *crema*.

Vegetable oil for frying
16 day-old yellow corn tortillas
Salsa Roja (recipe follows), kept warm
Shredded Beef (page 97) or Picadillo (page 70)

TO SERVE
Grated cotija or Monterey jack cheese
Mexican crema or sour cream
Shredded lettuce
Diced red or white onion

Pour 1/8 inch of oil in a small frying pan and heat over medium-high heat. Working in batches, fry the tortillas, turning once, until they start to brown around the edges but are still flexible, adding oil to the pan as needed between batches. Allow the oil to drip off and immediately dip the tortilla into the hot Salsa Roja. Fill each tortilla with about 1/4 cup of the hot beef, roll up, and serve immediately, sprinkled with a little cheese and topped with a dab of *crema*, shredded lettuce, and some onion.

Salsa Roja

MAKES 3 CUPS

20 large mild guajillo chiles, stemmed and seeded
3 cups hot water
1 teaspoon whole cumin seeds
1/4 teaspoon whole black peppercorns
1 teaspoon whole dried Mexican oregano
2 teaspoons vegetable oil
1/2 white onion, finely minced
5 cloves garlic, finely minced
1 teaspoon kosher salt
2 1/2 cups water or Caldo de Pollo (page 95), plus more as needed

Heat a heavy skillet over medium-high heat. Working in batches, add a few chiles and toast on both sides, turning occasionally and pressing down with a spatula, until they soften and blister. Remove from the pan. When the chiles are cool enough to handle, tear them into small pieces and place in a heatproof bowl. Add the hot water and soak the chiles, stirring occasionally, for 15 minutes. Drain, reserving 1 1/2 cups of the soaking liquid.

In a blender, combine the chiles and the reserved soaking liquid and puree for several minutes, or until perfectly smooth, scraping down the sides several times.

In a small skillet over medium heat, toast the cumin, peppercorns, and oregano until fragrant, stirring frequently so they don't burn. Let cool completely and grind in a spice grinder.

Heat the oil in the large skillet over medium heat. Add the onion, garlic, and ground spices and cook, stirring, until onions are softened, about 5 minutes. Add the chile puree and cook, stirring, until the salsa thickens and sizzles in the pan, 10 to 15 minutes. Add the salt and water, stir thoroughly, and simmer for 10 minutes. Add more water, if necessary, until the salsa is just thick enough to cling to a spoon.

Before serving, taste and adjust the seasoning.

Enmoladas de Pollo

CHICKEN WITH MOLE NEGRO ↓ Makes 16 enmoladas

In Mexican cooking, if you use a different sauce the name of the dish changes. In this recipe, instead of using a sauce made with *chiles* (which would give us en*chil*adas), I dip the tortillas in a sumptuous *mole,* which gives us en*mol*adas. *Enmoladas* are a good reason to make extra mole and a wonderful way to use up leftovers. Enmoladas are usually folded in half, rather than rolled.

Mole Negro (page 41), kept warm
Vegetable oil for frying
16 day-old corn tortillas
1 cup grated Chihuahua (menonita) or
    Monterey jack cheese

TO SERVE
1/8 cup Mexican crema or sour cream
Toasted sesame seeds
Diced white onion

If you haven't already done so, remove the skin and bones from the chicken in the mole and discard. Shred the meat into small pieces. In a bowl, stir together the chicken and enough mole sauce to moisten the meat (about 2 cups), keeping the rest of the sauce separate. Keep warm.

Pour 1/8 inch of oil in a small frying pan and heat over medium-high heat. Fry the tortillas, turning once, until they start to brown around the edges but are still flexible. Dip each tortilla in the hot mole sauce, fill with chicken and a bit of cheese, and fold in half.

To serve, top each *enmolada* with a spoonful of mole sauce, a teaspoon of *crema*, some sesame seeds, and a few pieces of diced onion. Serve immediately.

Burrito Ahogado

"WET" CHICKEN AND RICE BURRITO WITH FRESH TOMATO AND GUAJILLO SALSA ⤓ Serves 6

I love burritos and *tortas* served *ahogados,* "drowned" in a red chile sauce that is sometimes eye-wateringly spicy. These delicious burritos combine shredded chicken with rice, avocado, and lettuce, so eat it quickly before the lettuce loses its crunch. These burritos can be made with any smooth salsa, such as Salsa Roja (page 76), Salsa Verde (page 74), or even Roasted Tomato Salsa (page 69). Since the rice is already inside, you can serve it with just beans—Frijoles Negros (page 104) are especially good.

6 (12-inch) flour tortillas
Arroz Mexicana (page 101), kept warm
Shredded Chicken (page 97), kept warm
Roasted Tomato Salsa (page 69)
Diced white onions mixed with chopped fresh
　cilantro
2 Hass avocados, peeled and sliced
2 cups shredded lettuce
1 cup (6 ounces) grated cotija cheese, plus
　more for serving
Fresh Tomato and Guajillo Salsa (recipe follows),
　kept warm

TO SERVE
　Chopped fresh cilantro
　Chopped green onions

Heat a large, heavy skillet or griddle over medium-high heat. One at a time, heat the tortillas in the skillet, turning once and pressing down with a spatula, until warm and lightly toasted on both sides.

Lay a tortilla on a plate and spoon $1/2$ cup of the rice in the center, leaving 2 inches uncovered on each side and 3 inches uncovered on the top and bottom. Top with $1/2$ cup of the chicken, $1/4$ cup of the Roasted Tomato Salsa, and 2 tablespoons of the onion and cilantro mixture. Arrange a sixth of the avocado slices down the center and add a sixth of the lettuce. Sprinkle with 2 tablespoons of the cotija.

Fold in both sides to partly cover the filling. Fold the bottom up and tuck it firmly over the filling, then roll up the burrito snugly to form a tight cylinder. Repeat with the remaining ingredients.

Set each burrito on a serving plate and ladle over $1/2$ cup (or more, if you like) of the Fresh Tomato and Guajillo Salsa.

To serve, sprinkle each burrito with a little cheese, the cilantro, and the green onions. Serve immediately.

continued

Fresh Tomato and Guajillo Salsa

MAKES ABOUT 4½ CUPS

This excellent salsa balances earthy dried chiles with the sweetness of tomatoes and tart tomatillos. It may be substituted for any of the cooked salsas used in any of the recipes in this book. This makes a mildly spicy sauce. If you want a hotter salsa, add as many as 10 more chiles de árbol.

8 guajillo chiles, stemmed and seeded
4 ancho chiles, stemmed and seeded
4 chiles de árbol, stemmed and seeded
2 tablespoons fresh lard or vegetable oil
½ small white onion, minced
4 large cloves garlic, minced
3 Roma tomatoes, diced
2 tomatillos, husked, washed, and diced
1 teaspoon whole dried Mexican oregano
3 cups water or Caldo de Pollo (page 95),
   or more as needed
1½ teaspoons kosher salt
¼ teaspoon freshly ground black pepper

Tear all the chiles into small pieces. In a large skillet, heat the lard over medium-high heat. Add the chiles, onion, and garlic and cook, stirring often, until the onions begin to soften, about 5 minutes. Add the tomatoes, tomatillos, and oregano and cook, stirring, until the tomatoes are soft and the skillet is dry, 5 to 7 minutes. Add the water, salt, and pepper and simmer for 10 minutes. Transfer to a blender and puree until smooth. For a velvety texture, pass the sauce through a food mill to remove any remaining skins and fibers, or use as is. The salsa should just cling to a spoon. If necessary, thin with a little more water. Taste and adjust the seasoning and use hot.

Burrito "El Güero"

BEEF AND BEAN BURRITO WITH CHEESE ↓ *Serves 6*

Have you noticed that burritos keep getting bigger? This hefty creation is as much an American classic as the hamburger, a big, sloppy "bro-rito" in the best over-the-top tradition. (The teasing title's literal translation is White Guy Burrito.) But it's all in good fun. Be careful about how much of each filling ingredient you use or your burrito will wind up the size of a dirigible and fall apart in your lap. Slice each burrito into four pieces to serve a bigger group.

6 (12-inch) flour tortillas
2 cups grated Chihuahua (menonita) or
    Monterey jack cheese
Frijoles Puercos (page 106)
Shredded Beef (page 97) or Carne con
    Chorizo y Papas (page 51)
3/4 cup diced white onion mixed with chopped
    fresh cilantro
Salsa Mexicana (recipe follows)
2 sliced Hass avocados
3/4 cup sliced pickled jalapeños
3/4 cup sour cream

Heat a large, heavy skillet or griddle over medium-high heat. One at a time, heat the tortillas in the skillet, pressing down with a spatula, until warm and lightly toasted on one side. Turn the tortilla over and scatter 1/3 cup cheese over the tortilla, leaving 2 inches uncovered around the edges.

When the cheese is melted, lay the tortilla on a plate and spoon 1/2 cup of the beans across the center, leaving 2 inches uncovered on each side and a bit more space on the top and bottom. Top with 1/2 cup of the beef mixture, 2 tablespoons of the onion and cilantro mixture, and 2 tablespoons the salsa. Arrange a sixth of the avocado sliced down the center, then 2 tablespoons of the pickled jalapeños, and finally spoon 2 tablespoons sour cream evenly down the middle.

Fold in both sides to partly cover the filling. Fold the bottom up and tuck it firmly over the filling, then roll up the burrito snugly to form a tight cylinder. Repeat with the remaining ingredients and serve immediately.

Salsa Mexicana

MAKES ABOUT 2 1/2 CUPS

This simple fresh tomato salsa adds fresh taste and crunch to almost anything. Make sure it is well seasoned.

4 Roma tomatoes, finely diced
1/4 white onion, finely diced
1 serrano chile, stemmed, minced
1 teaspoon kosher salt
8 sprigs fresh cilantro, chopped
Juice of 1/2 lime

Combine all of the ingredients in a small bowl and stir well.

Burrito de Carnitas

BRAISED PORK BURRITO WITH SALSA VERDE AND AVOCADO-TOMATO SALSA ↙ Serves 6

All the flavors work together extremely well in this burrito, which is composed of layers of full-flavored pork, rice, tart salsa, crunchy onion, and chunks of avocado and *chicharrón*. The Avocado-Tomato Salsa—not a guacamole, but more like a chunky salad—is just as good in any of the burritos. Serve with the beans of your choice from Basics, Rice, Beans, and Other Sides (page 93), though Frijoles Negros (page 104) are the hands-down favorite in my house. The burrito is also delicious with Roasted Tomato Salsa (page 69) instead of the Salsa Verde.

Carnitas (page 98)
6 (12-inch) flour tortillas
Arroz Mexicana (page 101) or Arroz Verde
   (page 101), kept warm
Salsa Verde (page 74), kept warm
Avocado-Tomato Salsa (recipe follows)
3/4 cup diced white onions mixed with chopped
   fresh cilantro
6 tablespoons crumbled chicharrón (optional)

Preheat the oven to 350°F. Reheat the carnitas in its cooking liquid, uncovered, until it begins to brown, 15 to 20 minutes. Remove all bits of visible fat from the meat.

Heat a large, heavy skillet over medium-high heat. One at a time, heat the tortillas in the skillet, turning once and pressing down with a spatula, until warm and lightly toasted on both sides.

Lay a tortilla on a plate and spoon 1/3 cup of the rice across the center, leaving 2 inches uncovered on each side and a bit more space on the top and bottom. Top with 1/2 cup of the Carnitas, 1/4 cup of the Salsa Verde, 1/3 cup of the Avocado-Tomato Salsa, and 2 tablespoons of the onion and cilantro mixture. Scatter about 1 tablespoon *chicharrón* pieces, down the middle.

Fold in both sides to partly cover the filling. Fold the bottom up and tuck it firmly over the filling, then roll up the burrito snugly to form a tight cylinder. Repeat with the remaining ingredients and serve immediately.

Avocado-Tomato Salsa

MAKES 3 CUPS

The avocado should be ripe but still firm. This salsa keeps well, but you likely won't have any leftovers.

3 large, ripe Hass avocados
1/2 teaspoon kosher salt
Juice of 1/2 lime
1/2 cup diced red or white onion
1 Roma tomato, diced
10 sprigs fresh cilantro, chopped

In a small bowl, combine all the ingredients. Taste and adjust seasoning, if necessary.

Burrito con Carne Colorado "El Norte"

BURRITO WITH BEEF IN SPICY RED CHILE SAUCE ⤵ Serves 6

Sun-dried *chiles colorado* infuse the cooking of the US Southwest and northern Mexico with the earthy flavor of sun-baked mountains and desert. North of the border, these smooth-skinned chiles are called New Mexico chiles. They have a nice balance of heat and fruitiness that is quite distinct from chiles of similar appearance. Hunt down chiles grown in Mexico or New Mexico for this recipe (and always avoid Asian and South American chiles, which might look similar but don't have the right flavor). This recipe, which can be made with either beef or pork, is medium-hot, with a pleasant slow burn. Serve with Arroz Mexicana (page 101) and Frijoles de Olla (page 104) or Frijoles Charros de Nuevo León (page 109).

CARNE COLORADO

8 dried New Mexico chiles, stemmed and seeded
8 large mild guajillo chiles, stemmed and seeded
6 cups hot water
4 large cloves garlic
3 teaspoons kosher salt
2 teaspoons whole cumin seeds
1 teaspoon whole black peppercorns
2 whole cloves
1 tablespoon fresh lard or vegetable oil
2½ pounds lean beef chuck or pork shoulder, cut into ¾-inch pieces
2 teaspoons white vinegar

TO SERVE

6 (10-inch) flour tortillas
Diced red or white onions mixed with chopped fresh cilantro

Place the chiles in a heatproof bowl and pour the hot water over them. Let soak for 15 minutes, stirring once or twice. Drain, reserving 1½ cups of the soaking liquid.

In a blender, combine the chiles, the reserved soaking liquid, garlic, and salt and puree for several minutes until perfectly smooth, scraping down the sides several times.

In a small skillet over medium heat, toast the cumin, peppercorns, and cloves until fragrant, stirring frequently so they don't burn. Let cool completely and grind in a spice grinder.

Heat the lard in a large, heavy skillet over medium-high heat. Working in batches if necessary, brown the meat on one side without stirring, until it is dark brown. Turn the meat and brown the other side. Add the ground spices and cook for 1 minute. Transfer to a 5-quart slow cooker and add the chile puree. Stir, cover, and cook on low for 3 to 4 hours, or until the meat is tender. Stir in the vinegar.

To assemble the burritos, heat a large heavy skillet or griddle over medium-high heat. One at a time, heat the tortillas in the skillet, turning once and pressing down with a spatula, until warm and lightly toasted on both sides. Lay a tortilla on a plate and spoon ¾ cup of the meat mixture down the center, leaving 2 inches uncovered on each side and 3 inches open on the top and bottom. Scatter a bit of the onion and cilantro mixture over the meat. Fold in both sides to partly cover the filling. Fold the bottom up and tuck it firmly over the filling, then roll up the burrito snugly to form a tight cylinder. Repeat with the remaining tortillas and filling, and serve immediately.

TAMALES 101

The tamal is *the* iconic Mexican food. It has been made in various forms for thousands of years in nearly every region of the country. Only a few basic ingredients are involved, but they must be handled correctly to make a masa that will both be tender *and* hold together. Most difficult of all is the cooking, for tamales have to be cooked just right, with a consistent temperature and moist heat. Cooking them in a traditional stove top *tamalero* steamer can be tricky, as it demands that you nurse along a steamer of boiling water and hope that the water doesn't evaporate, all without being able to peek, which drops the temperature and makes the tamales heavy. Too *much* steam also results in leaden tamales. As it turns out, the even, moist heat of the slow cooker is ideal for slowly steaming the rich tamal masa to tender, fluffy perfection, and it's worry-free, too; you can leave it alone for a few hours with a clear conscience.

If you are going to the trouble of making tamales, you may as well make a lot. They freeze well, though there never seems to be that many left over. Tamales are an ideal social cooking project. Invite a few friends to your home or recruit your family to help you fill, fold, and tie the dozens of corn husk packets. Torta de Tamal (page 90) is the answer if you want to enjoy the taste of tamales without the fuss of wrapping and steaming them individually. If you happen to have some extra *guisados* tucked away in the freezer, this is one of the easiest recipes in the book to assemble.

Let's explore the tamal-making process.

Tamal Wrappers

Dried corn husks *(hojas)* are available in packages at Mexican markets, usually near the produce area. One package will include both large and small husks and usually makes about 50 tamales (you will overlap the smaller husks to make wraps of the appropriate size).

Any type of tamal can be wrapped in banana (plantain) leaves instead of corn husks, forming square and flat little packages. The leaves, which are usually available fresh in Latin or Mexican markets, impart a subtle, pleasant aroma to the tamales as they cook. Banana leaves are very long— 4 to 6 feet—and are sold rolled up. Package size varies from store to store and from fresh to frozen, but assume you will get about 8 (12-inch) squares per pound of banana leaf.

continued

Frozen banana leaves, which are sold in some Latin and many Asian (especially Filipino) markets, can also be used. They should be rinsed and dried, but they don't need to be toasted before using them. They look darker than fresh leaves, but they will taste exactly the same.

Preparing Corn Husk Wrappers

To prepare corn husks for wrappers, remove them from the package and gently loosen them from one another, but keep them aligned in their stack. Place the husks in a large bowl and soak in several changes of hot water for a total of 15 minutes, pushing them down gently to make sure the water penetrates the whole bundle. Drain well. If they seem gritty, rinse each husk individually after soaking and then drain again.

Preparing Banana Leaf Wrappers

To prepare banana leaves for wrappers, carefully unfold the banana leaf and, using scissors, remove the tough fiber along the top and bottom. Tear the leaf into 12-inch pieces, then rinse and wipe dry. To make tough leaves flexible, draw them quickly across a gas flame on both sides until shiny and soft. Using scissors, cut the leaves into 10-inch squares.

Tamal Masa

Tamal masa is prepared (moist) corn masa mixed with seasonings and leavening and beaten into well-whipped fat such as fresh lard (*asiento*) or vegetable shortening.

Premade tamal masa is often available at Mexican markets, especially around December, or it can be ordered from a *tortillería*. The problem with this is that you have no idea what's in it or how well it will work. I have consistently good results making my own masa using Maseca brand masa harina, which is readily available.

Masa made with vegetable shortening is the easiest to handle but has little flavor. Using *asiento,* which is more liquid, produces a softer masa. It's trickier to handle but aromatic and delicious. I like the results I get by using half vegetable shortening and half *asiento*: the masa is easy to work with and the pork flavor is authentic but not overpowering. (Do not substitute hydrogenated white lard, which is sold in 1-pound packages, for the *asiento*. The taste is not the same.) To combine, beat the vegetable shortening first, until creamy, then whip in the *asiento* a little at a time. Tamales made with too little fat will be dry and hard, and vegetable oil cannot be substituted for the solid vegetable shortening or lard.

Whichever type of fat you choose, make sure it is very cold and whip it until it is creamy and fluffy before combining it with the other ingredients. Add the prepared masa a few tablespoons at a time and blend well before adding more.

Tamal Fillings

Most tamales contain only a couple tablespoons of filling enrobed in the masa. The filling should be flavorful and quite thick, so you may need to cook it down in a skillet, stirring constantly, before using it. The meat should be in small pieces or shreds so that it is easier to handle and to eat.

Almost any combination of meat and salsa is good in a tamale, so don't hesitate to invent your own combinations. The classics are listed with the recipe on page 88.

Cooking Tamales

Tamales must be steamed over boiling water in a perforated vessel. Ideally, you will be able to find (or fabricate) a cake rack, bamboo basket, colander, or other perforated holder that fits snugly into your slow cooker. I use a sturdy disposable aluminum foil pie tin that I've poked full of holes about $1/2$ inch apart with a metal skewer. The round pie tin fits perfectly in my round slow cooker, or I can bend it to fit my oval cooker.

Set three upended metal or ceramic ramekins in the cooker to hold the rack over the surface of the water. This allows steam to circulate freely beneath the holder and up into the tamales.

Once you have set up your slow cooker with the rack and ramekins, figure out how much water you need to add to keep the level $1/2$ inch below the rack. Turn the cooker on high and add boiling water until it reaches that level. Set the ramekins and rack into the cooker and cover the rack with a single layer of overlapping corn husks. (A perforated surface, such as a colander or pie tin, does not need to be lined.) Cover the cooker and allow it to preheat while you make the tamales.

Stand the filled tamales on end in the slow cooker, arranging them in circles or in rows. They should be packed tightly enough that they stand on end, but loosely enough so that you can easily remove one for testing. You should be able to cook twelve to twenty tamales at a time in a 6-quart or larger oval cooker.

Cover the tamales with another layer of corn husks, tucking the ends down the sides. Thoroughly wet a kitchen towel and wring it out. Cover the cornhusks with the towel and tuck the ends down the side. Cook, covered, according to recipe instructions.

Tamales

Makes 36 to 48 tamales

In Mexico, tamales are often eaten out of their husks without any salsa early in the day, sometimes accompanied by a cup of Mexican chocolate or a corn *atole*. Later in the day, a tamal may be served with a meat entrée, along with rice and beans, or cloaked in a rich mole sauce.

Leftover tamales can be fried and tucked into a toasted *torta* roll along with lettuce, *crema,* and tomatoes to make the Mexico City specialty *guajolote* (literally, "turkey"). I have also seen tacos made from tamales, and deep-fried tamales are not unheard of. Leftover tamales can be reheated in their husks in the microwave or in a frying pan. They also freeze well—though we never have enough left over to bother.

1 (8-ounce) package dry corn husks, or 2 pounds banana or plantain leaves

MASA FOR TAMALES
3 cups dry masa harina (preferably Maseca brand)
2 teaspoons baking powder
1 teaspoon kosher salt
2 cups warm water
3/4 cup cold vegetable shortening
1/2 cup cold fresh lard
1 cup chilled Caldo de Pollo (page 95)

FILLING OPTIONS
Shredded Chicken (page 97) and Salsa Verde (page 74)
Carne Colorado (page 83)
Pork Carnitas (page 98) and Salsa Verde (page 74) or Salsa Roja (page 76)
Chorizo (straight from the package)
Carne con Chorizo y Papas (page 51)
Roasted poblano chiles (see page 5), torn into strips, and pieces of Chihuahua (menonita) cheese
Frijoles Refritos (page 105) with or without cheese

Prepare a slow cooker with a steaming rack as described in Cooking Tamales, page 86, and prepare the corn husk or banana leaf wrappers as described on page 86.

In a large bowl, whisk together the masa harina, baking powder, and salt until well blended. Add the water all at once and mix with a spoon or your hands until evenly moistened.

In a large bowl, combine the vegetable shortening and lard. With an electric hand beater or stand mixer, whip on medium speed until fluffy and creamy, 3 to 5 minutes. Add the masa 1/4 cup at a time, beating until smooth after each addition. Beat in the cold broth a few tablespoons at a time.

To assemble the tamales using corn husks, spread a clean kitchen towel on a work surface. Spread out one of the prepared corn husks. Dollop about 1/4 cup of masa in the center of the husk and spread it to within 1 inch of the sides, 2 inches of the bottom, and 3 inches of the top (the pointed end) of the husk. Place 2 tablespoons or less of filling down the center of the masa. Fold over the sides of the husk securely but not too tightly so the masa covers the filling. Fold the bottom husk up, then the top down over the bottom flap. Tie loosely with a strip of husk.

To assemble the tamales using banana leaves, spread a rectangle of masa in the center of a prepared square, leaving space around it on all sides. Place the filling down the center of the masa. Fold the leaf so the masa folds over on itself to enfold the filling. Turn up the sides to form a flattish square and tie with string.

Fill the cooker with tamales and cover with a layer of corn husks and a damp towel, as described in Cooking Tamales, page 86. To steam the tamales wrapped in banana leaves, arrange them in the steamer in flat layers rather than on end.

For both styles of tamales, cover the cooker and cook the tamales on high until one plucked from the center is fairly firm and bouncy or a little spongy. This may take $3^1/_2$ to 4 hours or longer, depending on the size of the tamales, your cooker, and how often you peek. (It's best if you don't open the cooker before the 3-hour mark.) Tamales made with lard will be a little softer than those made with shortening.

The tamales may be kept warm in the cooker on low for several hours. Keep covered.

Torta de Tamal

TAMAL PIE ⭿ **Serves 6**

Essentially one giant tamal, this dish gives you all the great flavor of a tamal without the fuss of wrapping them individually. I prefer to think of making this dish as being practical, not lazy. *Torta de tamal* is a terrific party or buffet dish; just cut it into squares to serve. For filling, I particularly like to use Carne Colorado (page 83), Carne con Chorizo y Papas (page 51), or Shredded Chicken (page 97) moistened with Salsa Verde (page 74).

¼ cup vegetable shortening
½ package dried corn husks, soaked (see
   page 86), or 4 (12-inch) squares fresh
   banana leaf, toasted (see page 86)
Masa for Tamales (page 88)
4 cups of your choice of tamale filling

With the shortening, liberally coat the bottom and sides of a 5- or 6-quart slow cooker insert. Line the bottom and two-thirds of the way up the sides with the corn husks or banana leaves, slightly overlapping the edges. Place half of the masa in the bottom of the cooker and spread evenly to the edges and ½ inch up the sides of the insert. Cover evenly with the filling. Spread the remaining masa over the filling.

Cover the masa with a layer of corn husks or a piece of banana leaf. Cover and cook on low for 4 hours, or until a knife inserted into the center comes out clean. The *torta* may be served at once or kept warm for several hours on low heat.

Basics, Rice, Beans, and Other Sides

Caldo de Pollo • 95
CHICKEN BROTH

Caldo de Res • 96
BEEF BROTH

Shredded Chicken • 97

Shredded Beef (Barbacoa) • 97

Carnitas • 98
SLOW-COOKED PORK

Arroz al Vapor • 99
STEAMED RICE

Arroz Mexicana • 101
RICE WITH FRESH TOMATO

Arroz Verde • 101
RICE WITH GREEN CHILES AND CILANTRO

Frijoles de Olla • 104
BASIC PINTO BEANS

Frijoles Negros • 104
BLACK BEANS

Frijoles Refritos • 105
REFRIED BROWN OR BLACK BEANS

Frijoles Puercos • 106
REFRIED BEANS WITH CHEESE AND PORK

Ayocotes • 107
BLACK BEANS WITH RED CHILES

Frijoles Charros de Nuevo León • 109
BEANS WITH BEEF, CHIPOTLES, AND EPAZOTE

Pan de Elote • 110
SLOW COOKER CORN BREAD

Elotes • 113
SIMMERED FRESH CORN WITH EPAZOTE,
CHILES, BUTTER, AND LIME

Chiles en Escabeche • 114
TEQUILA-PICKLED JALAPEÑOS AND VEGETABLES

Although these basic Mexican dishes are simple to make, they're anything but ordinary. You will turn to this chapter again and again for directions on making shredded beef, pork, and chicken that can be used in all sorts of dishes, as well as other simple recipes to add authentic Mexican flavor to your meal.

Caldo (stock or broth) is the foundation for great flavor in all your cooking. It's the basis for hearty homemade soups, but it's also used to add rich flavor to *guisados*, salsas, and rice. And using the slow cooker, creating a clear, delicious stock is practically effortless.

No Mexican meal is complete without rice and beans, and here I go beyond the plain pinto bean to explore an array of delicious bean preparations from all over Mexico. Why settle for plain brown beans, as good as they are, when you can have the black beans with red chiles, which are popular in San Luis Potosí, in central Mexico's high desert, or you can indulge in the heart-stoppingly rich Frijoles Puercos (page 106) from Mazatlán?

Surprise! You'll also learn your slow cooker doubles as a rice cooker, oven, and *escabeche* (pickle) maker. Other authentic additions to your table found in this chapter include a lovely corn bread wrapped in corn husks (Pan de Elote, page 110) and a quick recipe for making Chiles en Escabeche (page 114).

All of these basic preparations, including the rice, freeze beautifully. So when you fire up the slow cooker, make enough for several meals and tuck the extras away in the freezer. You'll be glad you did.

Caldo de Pollo

CHICKEN BROTH ⭳ Makes 12 cups

Using the slow cooker to make broth is much easier than fussing over a stockpot, and it yields perfect broths that are clear and delicious. You can use this simple broth, with its light flavor and golden color, to enrich a multitude of simple soups and rice dishes. Since the broth freezes beautifully, always keep some on hand so you have a head start whenever you want to make homemade soup. That alone is a good reason in invest in a 6- or 7-quart slow cooker, even if you usually only cook for two.

1 small carrot, peeled and diced
1 celery stalk, diced
1 large white onion, diced
10 sprigs fresh flat-leaf parsley or fresh cilantro
1 tablespoon kosher salt
1 large clove garlic, halved
2 dried bay leaves
1 teaspoon whole black peppercorns
1 ancho chile, stemmed, seeded, and toasted (see page 6)
3 pounds meaty chicken wing tips or backs and necks
12 cups water

Combine all the ingredients in a 6- or 7-quart slow cooker. Cover and cook on low for 8 hours. Remove the lid, turn off the cooker, and allow the broth to cool and settle for 30 minutes.

Set a colander over a large bowl. Using a slotted spoon or skimmer, carefully lift all the solids from the cooker without scraping the bottom and drain them in the colander. Use a ladle or large measuring cup to remove the remaining broth from the slow cooker and pass through the colander. (Be careful not to disturb any of the small bits on the bottom; these will make the broth cloudy. Pour the last remnants of the broth and the bits on the bottom into a separate container and discard.) Do not press down on the solids in the colander, but allow the broth to drain on its own for 15 minutes. Once it has stopped dripping, discard the solids in the colander. Let the broth cool to room temperature and then chill. Before freezing it or using it in a recipe, remove any layer of fat that floats to the surface.

VARIATION

• To turn this broth into a quick and simple soup, substitute a whole chicken or 3 pounds of chicken pieces for the wing tips. Cook, covered, on low for 8 hours, then strain and defat the broth as described above. Remove the skin and bones from the chicken and discard, then shred the meat. In large soup pot, combine the broth and shredded chicken and add diced carrots, corn, and any other vegetables you like, plus rice, noodles, or cooked garbanzo beans. Simmer on the stove top until the vegetables are cooked, about 30 minutes. Season to taste with salt before serving.

Caldo de Res

BEEF BROTH ⭤ Makes 12 cups

This recipe yields a light, clear beef broth that adds subtle flavor to *guisados*, soups, and sauces. The meat loses some of its flavor to the broth, but it can be shredded and then added to a soup such as Sopa de Fideos (page 26), used in any of the bean recipes, or added to tacos or burritos.

2 Roma tomatoes, quartered
$1/2$ white onion, diced
2 cloves garlic, peeled
1 jalapeño chile, stemmed and seeded (optional)
1 small carrot, peeled and diced
1 dried bay leaf
1 teaspoon kosher salt
$1/2$ teaspoon whole black peppercorns
1 guajillo chile, stemmed, seeded, and toasted
  (see page 6)
1 pound boneless beef chuck, in one piece
2 pounds meaty beef neck or shin bones
12 cups water

Combine all the ingredients in a 7-quart slow cooker. Cover and cook on low for 8 hours. Remove the lid, turn off the cooker, and allow the broth to cool and settle for 30 minutes. Remove the chuck in one piece and reserve for another use.

Set a colander over a large bowl. Using a slotted spoon or skimmer, carefully lift all solids from the cooker without scraping the bottom and drain in the colander. Use a ladle or large measuring cup to remove the remaining broth from the slow cooker and pass through the colander. (Be careful not to disturb any of the small bits on the bottom; these will make the broth cloudy. Pour the last remnants of the broth and the bits on the bottom into a separate container and discard.) Do not press down on the colander, but allow the broth to drain on its own for several minutes. Once it has stopped dripping, discard the solids in the colander. Let the broth cool to room temperature and then chill. Before freezing it or using it in a recipe, remove any layer of fat that floats to the surface.

NOTE
If you want plenty of leftover shredded beef to use in other recipes, double the amount of chuck, which will make the broth even tastier. Alternatively, the chuck may be left out altogether, though this will make a lighter-flavored broth.

Shredded Chicken

Enough for 12 tacos or enchiladas, 6 burritos, 24 quesadillas, or 24 tamales

This basic chicken recipe is used in Tacos de Pollo (page 66), Enchiladas Suizas (page 74), and Burrito Ahogado (page 79), among other dishes. To ensure a fresh-tasting dish, don't overcook the chicken.

3 bone-in chicken breasts or 2 pounds
    boneless chicken meat (breasts, thighs,
    or a combination)
1 cup water
1/2 white onion, diced
1 jalapeño or serrano chile, split lengthwise
1 1/2 teaspoons kosher salt

Combine all the ingredients in 4-quart slow cooker, cover, and cook on low for 3 to 4 hours, but no longer. Let cool until cool enough to handle, then discard the chicken bones and skin and shred the meat into small pieces. Strain the cooking liquid, discarding the solids, and reserve for another use. Use the shredded chicken immediately or refrigerate until needed.

Shredded Beef (Barbacoa)

Enough for 12 tacos or enchiladas, 6 burritos, 24 quesadillas, or 24 tamales

This incredibly tender beef can be used in Tacos de Res Dorado (page 69), Enchiladas en Salsa Roja (page 76), and Burrito "El Güero" (page 81), and many other dishes. For the best flavor, use select or choice boneless beef chuck (shoulder).

2 pounds boneless beef chuck, cut into
    large chunks
1 cup water
1/2 white onion, diced
1 Roma tomato, roasted (see page 133) or raw,
    chopped to a pulp
3 large cloves garlic, sliced
2 serrano chiles, split lengthwise
10 sprigs fresh cilantro
6 sprigs fresh epazote or 1 tablespoon dried
    epazote
2 1/2 teaspoons kosher salt

Combine all the ingredients in 5-quart slow cooker, placing the meat on top. Cover and cook on low for 4 hours, pushing the meat down into the broth several times. Turn off the slow cooker, uncover, and let the meat cool in the broth for 30 minutes. Remove the meat from the broth and shred it into small pieces. Strain the cooking liquid, discarding the solids, and reserve for another use. Use the shredded beef immediately or refrigerate until needed.

Carnitas

SLOW-COOKED PORK ⬇ **Enough for 24 tacos, 12 burritos, or 36 tamales**

Succulent, tender carnitas is easy to make, and so delicious that it could make you famous. Much of the rich flavor comes from the fat that renders into the cooking broth, but this is easily removed after chilling. Always allow the meat to cool in the cooking broth, which keeps it moist and flavorful. This recipe is used in Tacos de Carnitas (page 73), Burrito de Carnitas (page 82), Frijoles Puercos (page 106), and Tamales (page 88). Freeze any leftovers.

4 pounds boneless pork butt
1 cup water
2 teaspoons kosher salt

Cut the pork into 3-inch chunks and place in the slow cooker with the water and salt. Cover and cook on low for 7 to 8 hours, or until very tender. Turn off the slow cooker, uncover, and let the meat cool in the broth for 30 minutes. Remove the meat from the broth and carefully remove any large pieces of fat without breaking the meat up too much. Return the meat to the broth. Use the carnitas immediately or refrigerate it in its broth until needed. If you refrigerate it, remove the layer of white fat (*asiento*, see Note) before reheating.

NOTE
Don't trim the fat from the pork before cooking it. It renders out during cooking, enriching the flavor of the meat, and can easily be removed after chilling the carnitas. Reserve this pure white lard *(asiento)* and use it for sautéing meats such as Picadillo (page 70) or making any of the *guisados* in Mains and Guisados (page 35). Fresh lard is wonderful to cook with; it has amazing flavor and can be heated to high temperatures for effective browning.

Arroz al Vapor

STEAMED RICE ↙ Serves 6

As long as you make a few adjustments to your usual method for making rice, your slow cooker can double as a rice cooker. For the best results, use *converted* (which is *not* the same as instant) long-grain white or brown rice, which stays perfectly al dente and does not clump. Tossing the rice with a small amount of oil before cooking it also helps to keep the grains separate and fluffy. Regular long-grain white or brown rice works perfectly well, but it will require more experimentation, due to its variable size and moisture content, and it will also tend to be softer and stickier when cooked. If you're using regular rice, you may want to experiment with using slightly less water—as much 1 tablespoon less per cup of rice.

Normally rice is never stirred while it cooks. However, because the slow cooker heats from the sides in to the center, a good stir about 30 minutes into the process seems to help the rice cook more evenly. You should also turn the earthenware insert in your cooker 180 degrees after 1 hour, as cookers often heat unevenly.

At the end of the cooking time, when the rice has absorbed all the visible water, turn the cooker off but do not remove the lid or stir for 15 minutes. This will allow the rice to evenly absorb all the moisture remaining in the pot. After 15 minutes, remove the lid and gently fluff the rice with a fork or a single chopstick, stirring just enough to loosen the rice. (Don't use a spoon, which will crush the soft rice and make it gummy.) Let the rice continue to steam, uncovered, for another 15 minutes. At this point, the rice can be covered and the slow cooker turned on low to keep it warm.

2 cups converted white or brown long-grain rice
1 tablespoon vegetable oil
1 teaspoon kosher salt
4 cups water or Caldo de Pollo (page 95)

Place the rice in a 4- or 5-quart slow cooker. Add the oil and salt and stir thoroughly until each grain of rice is coated. Add the water, stir briefly, then make sure the rice is evenly distributed over the bottom of the cooker. Cover, and cook on high. After 30 minutes, gently stir the rice, and after 1 hour turn the earthenware insert 180 degrees.

After 2 hours total, turn off the cooker. Let stand, covered, for 15 minutes, then remove the lid and stir gently with a fork. Let the rice stand, uncovered, for another 15 minutes. At this point the rice is ready to be served. To hold, turn the cooker on warm or low, cover, and hold for up to 2 hours.

Arroz Mexicana

RICE WITH FRESH TOMATO ⩗ Serves 6

The classic accompaniment to Mexican food, *arroz mexicana* is delicately flavored with fresh tomato and a small amount of onion and garlic. For more tomato flavor, replace $1/2$ cup of the water with tomato juice.

2 cups converted white or brown long-grain rice
1 tablespoon vegetable oil
2 tablespoons finely chopped white onion
1 small clove garlic
1 teaspoon kosher salt
$1/2$ teaspoon ground cumin
3 Roma tomatoes
Water or Caldo de Pollo (page 95), as needed
$1/2$ cup frozen peas (optional)

Place the rice in a 5-quart slow cooker. Add the oil and stir thoroughly until each grain of rice is coated. Stir in the onion, garlic, salt, and cumin.

In a blender, puree the tomatoes. Add enough water or broth to bring the amount of liquid to 4 cups. Pour over the rice and stir well.

To cook the rice, cover and turn on high, stirring the rice after 30 minutes and turning the earthenware insert 180 degrees after 1 hour.

After 2 hours total, turn off the cooker. Add the peas to the slow cooker but do not stir. Replace the lid and let the rice stand, with the cover on, for 15 minutes, then remove the lid and stir gently with a fork. Let the rice stand, uncovered for another 15 minutes. Serve the rice right away. To hold, turn the cooker on warm or low and keep covered for up to 2 hours.

Arroz Verde

RICE WITH GREEN CHILES AND CILANTRO ⩗ Serves 6

Arroz verde gets its pale green color and smoky flavor from two kinds of charred green chiles and a healthy handful of fresh cilantro. Frying the vegetable puree and rice together enhances the flavor of the rice, but this step can be skipped if you're in a hurry.

2 poblano chiles, roasted (see page 5)
1 jalapeño chile, stemmed and seeded
$1/2$ small white onion, coarsely diced
1 tablespoon minced garlic
1 tablespoon kosher salt
1 bunch fresh cilantro, finely chopped
2 tablespoons vegetable oil
$2 1/2$ cups converted white or brown long-grain rice
3 cups water

Combine the chiles, onion, garlic, salt, and cilantro in a food processor. Pulse to form a smooth puree, scraping down the sides several times.

In a heavy skillet, heat the oil over medium heat. Add the uncooked rice and sauté, stirring often, until golden, about 5 minutes. Add the chile puree and cook, stirring, until absorbed. Transfer the rice to a 5-quart slow cooker. Pour the water over and stir well. To cook the rice, follow the cooking instructions for Arroz Mexicana, above.

BEANS

Along with rice, beans are a staple of the Mexican kitchen. Well-stocked Mexican markets sell dozens of kinds of beans, and even those that look similar might have different tastes and textures. There are three main types:

Brownish. Includes pinto, bayo, pink, golden peruviana (also known as peruana), flor de mayo, flor de junio, red (kidney), cranberry, and many local variations. When cooked, these beans are creamy-soft and mildly sweet.

Black. Some have white or reddish specks, some are flattish, and others are plump and round. They vary in size from tiny turtle beans to large *ayocotes*. Black beans tend to be more fibrous than brown but have a wonderful rich, almost smoky flavor. Fresh black beans are a staple of Mayan cooking in the Yucatán.

Habas. Habas are dried fava beans. (Their smaller, similar cousin, the *ibes* bean, is rather like a lima bean and is always used fresh.) These beans are flat, kidney-shaped, and pale in color with thick skins and crumbly, dry interiors.

Before cooking any type of bean, rinse them and pick them over carefully, discarding any stones or dirt you find. I always add a small amount of salt with the water, so the beans absorb the seasoning along with the liquid.

Cook beans until they are very soft when pressed between thumb and finger, making sure there is plenty of liquid in the cooker at all times. They will continue to absorb some of the cooking liquid and firm up as they cool.

Frijoles de Olla

BASIC PINTO BEANS ⤓ Makes 6 cups

Along with tortillas, humble *frijoles* are a staple at almost every meal in Mexico. That's not to say they are boring or predictable. There are many savory and satisfying ways of cooking beans, but I am perfectly happy with nothing more than some good pinto beans served with warm tortillas, some kind of fresh salsa, and a grating of salty cotija cheese. A great advantage of the slow cooker is that beans cook evenly and will not dry out. This recipe is good with typical medium-sized brownish beans, a category that includes not only pinto beans but also pink, red, mayocoba, peruviana, bayo, flor de mayo, and cranberry beans, as well as many other regional varieties. Serve these right from the slow cooker, make a batch of Frijoles Refritos (page 105), or freeze them.

2¹/₂ cups dried pinto or other beans
   (about 1 pound), rinsed and picked over
7¹/₂ cups water
1¹/₂ teaspoons crushed red pepper, or
   6 chiles de árbol (optional)
1 tablespoon kosher salt
1 teaspoon freshly ground black pepper

Combine all the ingredients in a 5-quart slow cooker, cover, and cook on low for 8 to 10 hours, or until the beans are very tender. (The timing depends on the age, type, and size of the bean.) There may be a fair amount of liquid left when the beans are done, but don't drain them—the beans will absorb most of it as they cool, becoming even more flavorful and creamy. Serve hot.

Frijoles Negros

BLACK BEANS ⤓ Makes 6 cups

Black beans are often associated with central and southern Mexico, but you will find them served in all parts of the country. In addition to having a distinct taste and texture, black beans are enhanced by cooking them with sprigs of fresh epazote, a leafy herb that adds a lovely minty-oregano flavor and reduces the gas that some people experience after eating too many beans. Black beans may be served whole *(de olla)*, as they are here, or mashed (see opposite).

2¹/₂ cups dried black beans (about 1 pound),
   rinsed and picked over
6 cups water
¹/₂ white onion, peeled, root end intact
3 chiles de árbol, stemmed
¹/₂ bunch fresh epazote sprigs, or
   2 tablespoons dried epazote
1 tablespoon kosher salt

Combine all the ingredients in a 5-quart slow cooker, cover, and cook on low 6 to 8 hours, until the beans are very tender. Cool in the cooking liquid. Remove the onion, chiles, and epazote sprigs. Serve hot.

Frijoles Refritos

REFRIED BROWN OR BLACK BEANS ⤓ *Serves 6*

Refried beans are usually mashed with plenty of fat, which makes them creamy and filling but a bit too rich for most people's taste. This lightened-up version uses a little fresh lard for flavor and plenty of the cooking liquid to make a smooth and delicious side dish. (If you want something richer, try the Frijoles Puercos on page 106.) Don't add salt to this dish; there is salt in the liquid used to cook the beans, and at any rate the beans should be a little underseasoned, to play off the big tastes of the entrees and salsas they usually accompany.

2 tablespoons fresh lard or canola or corn oil
1/4 cup finely minced white onion
1 small clove garlic, minced (optional)
4 cups cooked beans with their cooking liquid
Water or Caldo de Pollo (page 95), as needed

TO SERVE
Crumbled cotija cheese
Sliced green onions

In a large, heavy skillet, heat the lard over medium heat. Add the onion and garlic and cook, stirring, until softened, about 5 minutes.

Remove the skillet from the heat. Add 1 cup of the beans and their liquid to the pan and mash to a smooth paste (this will be easier if the beans are warm). Return the skillet to the heat and continue to add the remaining beans, 1 cup at a time, mashing them until smooth after each addition and adding liquid as needed. When all the beans are mashed, add any remaining cooking liquid (and additional water or broth, if necessary) to thin to the correct consistency. The beans should be thick but not stiff.

Serve hot, sprinkled with the cotija cheese and green onions.

VARIATION
• To make *frijoles borrachos* (literally, "drunken beans"), add 1/2 cup beer to the pan with the first cup of beans.

Frijoles Puercos

REFRIED BEANS WITH CHEESE AND PORK ↙ Serves 6

Sinaloa is famous for its wonderful seafood specialties, but I vividly remember the devastatingly rich, unctuous, pork-laden *frijoles puercos* (literally, "pork beans") that were served like clockwork at every meal, as if to balance out all that healthy fish. Dark brown and very smooth, *frijoles puercos* are beans mashed with soft Chihuahua cheese, pork, and more pork in the form of fresh rendered lard *(asiento)*, spicy chorizo, *chicharrón* (pork skin deep-fried in lard), bacon, shredded pork, and goodness knows what else as long as it once went "oink." Actually, to reframe Mae West's famous line, goodness has nothing to do with it. Keep the rest of the meal light.

½ cup shredded Carnitas (page 98; optional)
3 to 4 tablespoons fresh lard or bacon drippings
¼ cup very finely minced white onion
1 slice bacon, finely minced
½ cup pork chorizo, crumbled (about 5 ounces)
3 cups cooked pinto, bayo, or pink beans with
  their cooking liquid
¾ cup shredded Chihuahua (menonita) or
  Muenster cheese

TO SERVE
¼ cup crumbled chicharrón
⅓ cup sliced pickled jalapeño chiles
1 tablespoon toasted and crumbled guajillo chiles
  (see page 6)

Reheat the carnitas in its juices in a large uncovered skillet or in 350ºF oven until hot and a bit dry and crisp around the edges. Keep warm.

In a large skillet, heat the lard over medium heat. Add the onion and bacon and sauté until the onion is soft, about 5 minutes. Add the chorizo and cook, stirring, for about 10 minutes, or until the chorizo is well- browned and crumbly.

Add 1 cup of the beans and their liquid to the pan and mash to a smooth paste (this will be easier if the beans are warm). Return the skillet to the heat and continue to add the remaining beans, 1 cup at a time, mashing them until smooth and adding liquid as needed until the beans are very smooth and fairly thick.

Just before serving, stir the cheese into the beans, a little at a time, until the cheese is melted and absorbed by the beans. Spoon the beans into a serving dish. Top with the carnitas then sprinkle the *chicharrón,* jalapeños, and crumbled chiles on top. Serve hot.

Ayocotes

BLACK BEANS WITH RED CHILES ⤓ *Serves 6*

Large black beans with a purplish cast, *ayocotes* are the traditional bean to serve with tamales and rice dishes. This recipe was the star of a wonderful breakfast I had at an eighteenth-century saltworks in San Luis Potosí, along with hand-patted gorditas stuffed with chorizo and *chicharrón,* eggs cooked with nopales, heaps of *pan dulce,* and earthenware cups of strong coffee flavored with cinnamon and piloncillo sugar. This recipe is so flavorful that it's an excellent accompaniment to very simple foods, such as grilled or roasted meats. True *ayocotes* might be difficult to find outside of Mexico, but this recipe works perfectly well with regular black beans.

2 ancho chiles, stemmed and seeded
3 guajillo chiles, stemmed and seeded
4 chiles de árbol , stemmed and seeded
4 puya chiles, stemmed and seeded
1 1/2 cups hot water
1 tablespoon kosher salt
1 teaspoon freshly ground black pepper
2 Roma tomatoes, coarsely chopped
4 large cloves garlic
1 cup diced white onion
1 tablespoon whole dried Mexican oregano
2 1/2 cups dried black or ayocote beans
  (about 1 pound), rinsed and picked over
8 cups water

Heat a heavy skillet over medium-high heat. Add all the chiles and toast on both sides, turning occasionally and pressing down with a spatula, until they soften and blister. Remove from the pan. When the chiles are cool enough to handle, tear them into small pieces and place in a heat-proof bowl. Add the hot water and soak the chiles, stirring occasionally, for 30 minutes.

In a blender, combine the chiles and their soaking liquid, and the salt, pepper, tomatoes, garlic, onion, and oregano and puree until smooth. Pour into a 5-quart slow cooker.

Add the beans to the slow cooker and stir in the water. Cover and cook on low for 8 to 10 hours, or until very tender. Serve hot.

Frijoles Charros de Nuevo León

BEANS WITH BEEF, CHIPOTLES, AND EPAZOTE ↙ Serves 6

The *charro* (cowboy) lifestyle is alive and well in the beautiful mountains of northern Mexico. Here cooking often revolves around a big pot and a wood-fired cook box, where *frijoles* cook slowly overnight while the herd dozes under the stars. *Frijoles charros* always start with big handfuls of chipotles and epazote, and then, to paraphrase one cook, "you add whatever you got," whether it's chunks of beef, pigs' feet and skin, vegetables, or tomatoes. When cooked, the *frijoles* should be brothy but full of beans and pieces of meat. Serve with flour tortillas and, if you like, a spoonful of Salsa Mexicana (page 81).

2¹⁄₂ cups dried bayo, pinto, pink, or flor de mayo beans (about 1 pound), rinsed and picked over
1 tablespoon fresh lard or vegetable oil
1 pound boneless beef chuck, cut into ¹⁄₂-inch pieces
1 smoked pork hock or pig's foot, split
1 (7-ounce) can chipotle chiles in adobo
1 white onion, diced
4 Roma tomatoes, finely chopped, or 1 (14-ounce) can diced tomatoes in juice
2 jalapeño chiles, halved lengthwise
6 cloves garlic, sliced
10 sprigs fresh epazote, or 3 tablespoons dried epazote
2 teaspoons kosher salt
8 cups water

Place the beans in a large (at least 5¹⁄₂-quart) slow cooker.

In a large, heavy skillet, heat the lard over medium-high heat. Add the beef and brown on all sides, until it is a rich, deep brown. Transfer the beef to the slow cooker. Wrap the pork hock firmly in a piece of cheesecloth or tie with string;

this will allow the flavor to permeate the beans while keeping the small bones in one place. Add the pork to the cooker along with all the remaining ingredients. Cover and cook on low for 10 to 12 hours, or until the beans and meat are very tender. Remove and discard the epazote sprigs. Pick any meat from the pork hock and add to the pot.

VARIATION

• Browning the beef adds wonderful color and flavor to the dish, but if you don't have time, just add the cubed meat to the pot with the other ingredients.

NOTE

To add flavor and body to the finished dish, in addition to the pork hock or foot you may add a 6-inch square of fresh pig skin (available at well-stocked Latin butchers) or a 4-ounce piece of salt pork to the slow cooker along with the beans. Just before serving, cut into small pieces and return to the cooker.

Pan de Elote

SLOW COOKER CORN BREAD ⤓ *Serves 6*

Lightly sweetened with piloncillo sugar, corn bread is a favorite festival food in northern Mexico, where the batter is cooked in small cast-iron pans that are greased with plenty of sweet butter. Serve with more butter and a sprinkle of crushed piloncillo for a sweet treat, or offer it as a side dish to help temper the heat of a spicy *guisado* or entrée. This recipe, like that of all the cooks I spoke to, uses commercially available pancake mix. When I adapted the recipe to the slow cooker I tried using a homemade pancake mix, but it just didn't work as well.

$1/2$ cup salted butter

$2/3$ cup crushed piloncillo sugar or dark brown sugar

3 cups fresh corn kernels

1 cup water

$2^1/2$ cups dry pancake mix

Rub the bottom and sides of a 5-quart slow cooker with 1 tablespoon of the butter. Cut a piece of aluminum foil and line the bottom of the slow cooker, pressing it smoothly into the corners and halfway up the sides. Butter the foil with another 1 tablespoon of the butter.

Place the sugar in a heavy plastic bag and pulverize with a small cast-iron pan or wooden mallet. Add the crushed sugar to a blender along with the corn and water and pulse until just combined, leaving some chunks of sugar. Transfer the mixture to a bowl and stir in the pancake mix. Melt the remaining 6 tablespoons butter and stir into the batter.

Spoon the batter into the slow cooker. Drape a length of paper towel or a linen kitchen towel tightly across the cooker—this will absorb condensation that may form and drip onto the surface of the cornbread. Cover and cook on low for 4 hours or on high for $1^1/2$ to 2 hours, until the sides are well browned and a knife inserted in the center comes out clean. Serve hot.

VARIATIONS

- Stir in 1 cup of any combination of fresh corn kernels, diced onions, minced jalapeños, or grated cheese just before spooning the batter into the slow cooker.

- Add 1 tablespoon ground cinnamon to the batter, and sprinkle the top with $1/4$ cup pulverized piloncillo.

- For a dramatic presentation, instead of using aluminum foil, you can line the slow cooker with dried corn husks that have been cleaned and soaked as described on page 86. The golden bread set in a corona of corn husks looks terrific on a holiday table or buffet.

Elotes

SIMMERED FRESH CORN WITH EPAZOTE, CHILES, BUTTER, AND LIME ↙ Serves 4

Mexican farmers cultivate more than three hundred distinct varieties of corn, so it's no surprise that corn forms an integral part of the everyday Mexican diet. Fresh corn is a popular street treat, served from push-carts that are often just cauldrons of boiling water on wheels. The earthy-sweet flavor of the corn shines through the messy, delicious combination of butter, lime, salty cheese, creamy mayonnaise, and a sprinkle of mild chiles.

4 ears fresh corn
2 tablespoons salted butter
1 tablespoon kosher salt
3 sprigs fresh epazote

TO SERVE
Melted salted butter
Mild ground chiles, such as guajillo or
  ancho chile
Crumbled cotija cheese
Lime wedges
Mayonnaise

Shuck the corn and cut each cob into 3 pieces or leave whole. Combine the corn, water, butter, salt, and epazote in a 5-quart slow cooker. Cover and cook on low for $2^1/_2$ to 3 hours, stirring once. The corn may be held on warm for up to 2 hours more. To serve, drain the corn thoroughly. Pile the corn on a warm platter and drizzle with the butter. Sprinkle with a little of the ground chiles and cotija cheese. Serve with limes and and a small bowl of mayonnaise on the side.

Chiles en Escabeche

TEQUILA-PICKLED JALAPEÑOS AND VEGETABLES ⭹ Makes about 1 quart

This bright, crunchy combination of fresh vegetables and chiles *en escabeche* (which means pickled with spices and vinegar) will find a place on your table every day. The pickled jalapeños and vegetables add zest to *tortas,* burritos, tacos, salads, beans, and soup. Or just munch away on the chiles and vegetables between bites: they are an extraordinary palate cleanser. Aficionados of this addictive condiment know that cooking the jalapeños doesn't mellow their heat at all. Quite the opposite, it spreads the heat of the chiles, so that the carrot is often the spiciest vegetable in the bowl. Serrano chiles may be substituted, but they will have more heat and less chile flavor. The finished chiles will keep for several weeks in the refrigerator, and, in my opinion, they just keep getting better.

8 jalapeño chiles, halved lengthwise
5 small red Fresno chiles, halved lengthwise
3 small güero chiles, halved lengthwise
1/2 small head cauliflower, broken into
    1-inch pieces
1/2 chayote squash, cut into 1-inch pieces
1 carrot, peeled and sliced on an angle
1/2 white onion, cut into 1/2-inch strips
2 large cloves garlic, sliced
1 tablespoon kosher salt
2 dried bay leaves
1 teaspoon whole black peppercorns
1 teaspoon whole coriander seeds
6 whole cloves
2 tablespoons sugar
2 cups white vinegar
2 cups cider vinegar
2 tablespoons blanco tequila

Combine all the ingredients in a 5-quart slow cooker. Cover and cook on low for 2 1/2 hours, or until the vegetables are just tender when poked with the tip of a knife. Let cool, then cover and store in the refrigerator, leaving the vegetables in the pickling liquid.

Desserts

Arroz con Leche • 119
RICE PUDDING WITH CINNAMON

Arroz con Coco • 120
COCONUT RICE PUDDING

Pan y Chocolate • 123
MEXICAN CHOCOLATE BREAD PUDDING
WITH BANANAS

Dulce de Leche • 124

Dulce de Leche Flan • 125
FLAN WITH CARAMEL

Pan Dulce con Manzanas • 126
APPLE CAKE WITH CAFÉ DE OLLA SYRUP

Nothing demonstrates the impressive versatility of the slow cooker more than these easy dessert recipes. It is possible to simmer rice for *arroz con leche*, steam a bread pudding, cook flan in a hot water bath, and bake a cake, all in the same appliance.

Best of all, those of us who adore dulce de leche finally have a way to make it without having to watch the pot for hours.

A tradition of fine patisserie and baking exists in Mexico, though these treats are enjoyed almost exclusively outside the home, in tearooms and cafes. Most of the recipes in this chapter are quick home-style desserts that are not too rich and not too sweet, but just right after indulging in spicy food.

Desserts made in the slow cooker will be moister and a bit denser than those cooked in the oven. Draping a towel under the lid while baking or holding a dessert will absorb condensation that could drip down into the food.

Arroz con Leche

RICE PUDDING WITH CINNAMON ↓ *Serves 6*

This rich, creamy rice pudding is gently flavored by a small piece of true Saigon cinnamon bark, which is milder and sweeter than the cassia cinnamon used north of the border. Cinnamon figures prominently in both sweet and savory Mexican cooking. Every marketplace sells big bundles of rolled cinnamon bark quills, which are steeped in dark syrup for candied sweets, brewed with coffee to make *café de olla*, or toasted and ground for moles and *asados*. The cinnamon will turn the rice a pale caramel color as it cooks. If you like raisins in your rice pudding, add them for the last hour of cooking.

3/4 cup short-grain Arborio rice
1 cup heavy cream or evaporated milk
3 cups whole milk
1/8 teaspoon kosher salt
1/3 cup agave syrup
3 tablespoons sugar
1-inch piece Saigon cinnamon stick
1 teaspoon vanilla extract

SWEETENED WHIPPED CREAM
1 cup heavy whipping cream, chilled
2 tablespoons confectioners' sugar

To make the arroz con leche, combine all the ingredients except for the vanilla in a 4- or 5-quart slow cooker and stir to combine. Cover and cook on low for 2 1/2 hours, gently but thoroughly stirring the rice about every 30 minutes. When the rice is cooked, stir in the vanilla and remove the cinnamon stick. The pudding will thicken as it cools.

To make the sweetened whipped cream, pour the cream into a bowl. With an electric hand mixer or a stand mixer, beat the cream at medium speed until it begins to thicken, 3 to 5 minutes. Add the sugar and beat on medium-high speed until the mixture is thick and holds its shape.

Serve warm or cold, topped with a dollop of whipped cream.

Arroz con Coco

COCONUT RICE PUDDING ↓ Serves 6

Coconut lovers will adore this lush rice pudding flavored with both coconut milk and thick, sweet cream of coconut.

Serve small portions of the pudding accompanied by crunchy toasted coconut, fresh berries, or pineapple, or top it with whipped cream, toasted almonds, and crushed chocolate. For a variation, omit the other garnishes and grate a tiny bit of fresh lime zest on each serving. The pudding may be made vegan (though no less delicious) by substituting water, coconut juice, almond milk, or rice milk for the dairy.

1¼ cups coconut milk
1½ cups cream of coconut
1⅔ cups milk
¾ cup short-grain Arborio rice
Pinch of kosher salt

TO SERVE
Toasted coconut or toasted sliced almonds (optional)
Sweetened Whipped Cream (page 119)
Fresh berries or pineapple (optional)
Crushed Ibarra Mexican chocolate (optional)

Combine all the ingredients in a 4- or 5-quart slow cooker. Cover and cook on low for 2½ hours, gently but thoroughly stirring the rice about every 30 minutes. The pudding will thicken as it cools.

Serve warm or chilled, with any of the suggested garnishes.

Pan y Chocolate

MEXICAN CHOCOLATE BREAD PUDDING WITH BANANAS ⭷ Serves 6 to 8

This addictive bread pudding is a favorite at my SOL Cocina restaurants. The moist, cake-like pudding is studded with bananas that have been sautéed in brown sugar, and it is infused with the warm flavors of cinnamon, allspice, and cardamom, which flavor the Ibarra Mexican chocolate. Cracking the lid toward the end of the cooking time allows the pudding to firm up. You probably won't have leftovers, but if you do, be sure to refrigerate them; it's just as good cold.

3 tablespoons vegetable shortening
3 cups milk
1 1/2 cups granulated sugar
1 tablespoon vanilla extract
1 teaspoon ground cinnamon
1/2 teaspoon kosher salt
1 disk Ibarra Mexican chocolate, broken into pieces
2 cups semisweet chocolate chips
4 large eggs, beaten
2 tablespoons salted butter
2 ripe but firm bananas, peeled and diced
2 tablespoons dark brown sugar
8 cups cubed firm white bread

TO SERVE
Vanilla gelato
Fresh strawberries

Using half of the shortening, grease the bottom, corners, and halfway up the sides of the slow cooker insert. Line the insert with an 18-inch piece of aluminum foil, smoothing it carefully into the corners and against the sides. Grease the foil with the remaining shortening.

In a 2-quart saucepan over low heat, heat the milk, sugar, vanilla, cinnamon, and salt until the milk is steaming, but do not allow it to boil. Turn off the heat and stir in the Ibarra chocolate and 1 1/2 cups of the chocolate chips. Stir with a whisk until the chocolate has melted. Let cool to luke-warm, then whisk in the beaten eggs.

While the milk cools, melt the butter in a 10-inch skillet over medium heat. Add the bananas and brown sugar and sauté for several minutes, until the bananas are glazed.

Place the bread in a large mixing bowl. Add the chocolate mixture, the sautéed bananas, and the remaining 1/2 cup chocolate chips. Stir well.

Pour the bread pudding into the cooker, cover, and cook on low 4 to 4 1/2 hours, or until puffed and firm. For the last 30 minutes, open the lid a small crack to let excess steam escape. Uncover and let cool in the insert for 30 minutes. Serve from the cooker, or unmold onto a plate: Run a rubber spatula around the edges to loosen. Grasp the ends of the foil and lift out of the insert. Turn upside down, peel off the foil, and turn right side up onto a serving plate. Serve warm or cold, with a scoop of gelato on top and the strawberries alongside.

VARIATION
• If you have access to a Mexican *panadería*, you can make this dessert with churros instead of bread. Reduce the sugar to 1/2 cup and eliminate the cinnamon.

Dulce de Leche

Makes about 1¹/₄ cups

Like magic, sweetened condensed milk is transformed into a thick, luscious caramel while still in the unopened can. Of course, the slow cooker is ideal for this preparation, which must cook for several hours. If you like having dulce de leche around (and who doesn't?), you can cook as many as 3 or 4 cans at a time, depending on the shape and size of your slow cooker. Unopened and refrigerated, it keeps indefinitely. Just make sure the water can circulate freely between the cans and that the cans are always covered by an inch of boiling water. The longer you cook it, the darker and more delicious it becomes.

1 unopened (14-ounce) can sweetened condensed milk

Place the can in a slow cooker and cover with hot tap water by at least 1 inch (or more, if you plan on leaving it unattended for more than a few hours). Cook on high for 10 hours, checking the water level occasionally and topping off with boiling water from a kettle to keep the cans covered, if necessary. Tuck the corner of a kitchen towel under the edge of the lid to keep the lid from knocking as it boils. After 10 hours, turn the cooker off and let the can cool in the water. Store unopened in the refrigerator. After opening the can, transfer to a sealed storage container and use within several days. The dulce de leche may also be frozen in a freezer bag or plastic storage container.

VARIATION

- To make sweet and tangy *cajeta*, simply substitute a can of sweetened condensed goat's milk for the cow's milk.

Dulce de Leche Flan

FLAN WITH CARAMEL ↙ *Serves 6 to 8*

By finding a mold that will fit into your slow cooker and rigging up something to keep the bottom of the mold off the bottom of the slow cooker (I use chopsticks), you can use your slow cooker in place of an oven with a bain-marie. This darkly delicious flan is truly decadent. The secret to the depth of flavor and color is a long-cooked, deeply caramelized dulce de leche, which you should prepare the day before assembling this dessert. Serve with whipped cream and fresh seasonal berries.

2 tablespoons vegetable shortening
¾ cup sugar
5 large eggs
1 (12-ounce) can evaporated milk
Dulce de Leche (opposite) or
    1 (14-ounce) can store-bought
4 ounces cream cheese
1 teaspoon vanilla extract
¼ teaspoon kosher salt

TO SERVE
Sweetened Whipped Cream (page 119)
Fresh berries

Using the vegetable shortening, thoroughly grease a heatproof 6-cup mold that will fit in your 5 or 6-quart slow cooker. Place a rack or a few chopsticks in the bottom of the slow cooker to prevent the mold from resting on the bottom.

Place the sugar in a heavy saucepan and heat over medium heat until the sugar begins to melt. Swirl the sugar to combine the melted and unmelted portions, or stir with a wooden spoon, until the sugar is a dark golden brown, but not in danger of burning. Immediately pour the caramel into the bottom of the mold.

In a blender, combine the eggs, evaporated milk, dulce de leche, cream cheese, vanilla, and salt and blend until smooth. Pour into the mold. Set the mold on the rack in the slow cooker. Carefully pour boiling water into the slow cooker insert until it comes halfway up the sides of the mold.

Lay a clean kitchen towel tightly across the top of the cooker and hold snugly in place with the lid. This will prevent excess moisture from dripping into the flan as it cooks.

Cook on high until just firm and a skewer inserted comes out clean, about 2 hours. Remove the mold from the slow cooker and let cool on a rack, then chill, covered, for several hours or overnight.

Serve from the mold or unmold upside down on a plate. Serve cold garnished with the whipped cream and berries.

Pan Dulce con Manzanas

APPLE CAKE WITH CAFÉ DE OLLA SYRUP ↙ Serves 6 to 8

This unusual apple cake comes from the Mennonite country, near Chihuahua, in northern Mexico. The small amount of cheese makes the cake taste richer, and of course the combination of apples, nuts, and cheese is a classic. Use any mild firm white cheese, such as *asadero,* Chihuahua cheese, Muenster, mild Gouda, or Monterey jack. What makes this cake really special is the final drizzle of piloncillo-sweetened spiced coffee (*café de olla*) after cooking. The light molasses flavor and subtle hints of cinnamon and clove are the perfect finishing touch. This cake may also be made with pears, peaches, pineapple, ripe persimmons, or quince.

2 tablespoons vegetable shortening

9 tablespoons butter, softened

$^1/_3$ cup walnut pieces

2 green apples

1 tablespoon fresh lemon juice

2 tablespoons water

$^1/_2$ cup crushed piloncillo sugar

1 cup granulated sugar

2 large eggs, beaten

2 teaspoons vanilla extract

3 tablespoons sour cream

1 cup unbleached all-purpose flour

1 teaspoon baking powder

1 teaspoon ground cinnamon

$^1/_2$ teaspoon kosher salt

$^1/_2$ cup firm white cheese (see above), cut into small cubes

$^3/_4$ cup strong, hot coffee

1 cinnamon stick

1 whole clove

TO SERVE

Vanilla ice cream or sweetened whipped cream (optional)

To prepare the insert, use half of the shortening to grease the bottom, corners, and halfway up the sides. Line the insert with an 18-inch piece of aluminum foil, smoothing it carefully into the corners and against the sides. Grease the foil with the remaining shortening, using most of the shortening on the corners and sides.

Smear 3 tablespoons of the softened butter in a layer across the bottom of the insert. Scatter the walnuts over the butter.

Peel and core the apples and cut into thin slices. Arrange the sliced apples in overlapping slices on top of the butter. Pour the lemon juice and water over the apples. Sprinkle the apples lightly with 2 tablespoons of the piloncillo sugar.

In a mixing bowl, with an electric hand mixer, beat the remaining 6 tablespoons of the butter until creamy. Add the granulated sugar a little at a time, beating after each addition.

In a separate bowl, stir together the eggs, vanilla, and sour cream. Add the egg mixture to the butter mixture and beat until smooth.

continued

All rights reserved.
Published in the United States by Ten Speed Press, an imprint of
the Crown Publishing Group, a division of Random House LLC,
a Penguin Random House Company, New York.
www.crownpublishing.com
www.tenspeed.com

Ten Speed Press and the Ten Speed Press colophon are registered
trademarks of Random House LLC.

A cataloging-in-publication record has been established for
The Mexican Slow Cooker under the ISBN 978-1-60774-316-3

ISBN 978-0-385-36444-7

Printed in China

Design by Chloe Rawlins
Food styling by Kim Kissling
Prop styling by Ethel Brennan

10 9 8 7 6 5 4 3

First Hardcover Edition